C^RE

C∧RE

A property entrepreneur's perspective on building
and operating a successful care home business

MICHAEL CHITTENDEN

R3THINK PRESS

First published in Great Britain 2019
by Rethink Press (www.rethinkpress.com)

© Copyright Michael Chittenden

A donation from every sale of this book will be made to Race Against Dementia: https://raceagainstdementia .com/

Contents

Introduction

'To see a world in a mint ice cream...'

'To see a world in a grain of sand' goes the saying. And, in a similar vein, you can sum up the main message of this book through the following true, ice cream-related story.

A resident came to live in our care home from a neighbouring establishment – a lovely elderly gentleman whom I ended up getting to know well in the short time he was with us. We were sitting chatting about what we could do to make his time with us more enjoyable. 'I'd love a mint ice cream with my dinner,' he said, longingly. 'It's my favourite, but I've not had one since I left my own home. Where I stayed before, they only ever offered me vanilla, chocolate or strawberry.'

I was incredulous. He had been in a care home charging him £3,000 a month – an old man near the end of his life, a time when the pleasures start to be outnumbered by the pains – and no one had bothered to ask him what he would really like to have as his dessert.

As we had always accommodated every resident's personal preference in puddings, we had plenty of mint ice cream in stock. Sadly, the old gentleman was poorly and was only with us for a few months, but in that time he worked his way through quite a lot.

Why is his story so relevant?

My whole philosophy of caring for the elderly has been based on asking residents what we could do to make their lives not just more comfortable, but more enjoyable. And small details can mean a lot at this stage of a person's life.

It's not just about what you promise people in this business, it's all about what you deliver – and continue to deliver. Continuity and consistency require drive and passion.

And that's why this little story is at the heart of how you make your care home brilliant and successful: by listening to your residents, and continuing to listen, and fitting your 'systems' around them, not you.

This might sound like an obvious and simple solution, and in many respects it is. But achieving it requires a vision, a culture, a shared set of values clearly understood by everyone involved. In short, you need to establish ways of working that make excellence routine.

While designing and operating a care home has proved to be one of the most rewarding things I have ever done, I should explain that my heart is really in the property business. And as a businessman, I always look to make money from my investments.

So how is that consistent with delivering excellent care? Because I believe excellence and profitability can go hand in hand. And some of the world's best run and most profitable businesses have already proved that.

Over the past few decades I have invested in a wide array of different properties and sites, from flats to disused military stores, and from brownfield sites to hotels. With each I have sought to maximise the return I achieve on the investment, and usually (but not always) I have succeeded.

Making money is never easy. If it was, we'd all be rich. So, fortunately, I have learned as much from the setbacks as from the successes. This book is the first in a series recounting my personal experiences in property, explaining how anyone investing in one of the many different asset types can avoid the pitfalls and maximise their return – or 'sweat their asset', as the rather ugly phrase goes – through a philosophy of 'customer first'.

Having learned from my mistakes, I include them in this book, and hope they help you avoid making them too.

The turnaround moment in my life came with a book by Michael E Gerber called *The E-Myth Revisited*, which made me realise that good intentions and great entrepreneurial ideas on their own are not enough. At the heart of every successful business should be a highly systematic approach ensuring that every cog in an operation is performing to the very best of its ability and in synchronisation with every other cog.

Moreover, if you can establish a template for a successful care home, this can act as a model for more care homes to be equally profitable.

But this book is not about making as much money as one can from vulnerable people. In my view, maximising returns in property is not all about cutting corners and finding ways to trim costs at the expense of the customer experience. The single best way to generate a profit from property is to add value – turning something ordinary and quite possibly unappreciated into something exceptional and desirable.

That is the business model I established in my care home: I developed a 64-bed home based on principles of top quality care, and a near-£4 million investment was turned into a sale which almost doubled my investment in less than two years. My residents, meanwhile, enjoyed excellent care – and paid competitive rates for that positive experience.

The message of this book is this: there is absolutely nothing wrong with making a profit, but anyone going into the care industry should passionately want to provide (and continue to provide) an excellent service as well. And these two aims really are not incompatible. In fact, I would argue that the better the service you provide in the care sector, the more likely you are to gain financially. It's not a sector where you can cut corners or attempt to provide a service delivered down to a price. Ultimately, it won't just be the recipients of care who suffer, but you too.

Moreover, there is no reason why excellent care should be available only to those who can afford to pay a premium price. Another thread of this book is that many of the key ways to deliver quality care come from ensuring that staff and management are focused on giving every resident the best experience possible. That should not be the preserve of only the more expensive establishments.

A key principle of the care model I established in the home I set up was to treat residents both as individuals and as customers – customers who have paid a significant amount of money for the service they are receiving, and who have a choice in what they pay for and receive, rather than having to accept what is offered.

I wanted to bring the philosophy of running a hotel into my care home. The care element should be a given, while the hospitality provided should make residents feel as if their needs were anticipated and their custom never taken for granted.

To me, this is the mindset at the heart of good care.

In the early part of the book I describe my own personal journey, telling the story of how I came to set up my care home and the vision of good care that I was determined to deliver. I recognise that the care sector has moved on in many ways during the intervening years, but I believe the same principles apply. I follow this up with the advice I would give to anyone taking that same journey today.

The care sector is set to see massive growth in the years ahead, presenting huge opportunities for canny operators. But at present it is beset by equally massive problems – not least those of funding, quality concerns, and public perception and confidence.

I hope that by applying some of the lessons I have learned, more providers can make residential care a stage in people's lives that proves to be rich and rewarding rather than something to be dreaded and avoided if at all possible.

This book is my contribution to this very important debate.

CHAPTER 1

My Personal Journey Into Care

Inspiration comes from an unlikely place

Journeys can begin in the most unexpected of places. While I had done some research into the care sector previously, the event that spurred me into setting up a residential home took place in Perth, Western Australia – 9,000 miles away.

I was there on a holiday with my partner, who was visiting family. There is only so much time one can fruitfully spend with a partner's family, and so I took time off to walk around the city and surrounding areas, indulging in my favourite pastime of observing property.

I came across a nicely built complex and, at first, I assumed it was a holiday centre, or perhaps a hotel. I peered over the wall and thought how fantastic it looked – fountains, tropical plants, block-paved road. There were even golf buggies going about the place. It was like something out of *The Truman Show* – just fantastic.

I went in and the receptionist told me it was a care facility, which I found incredible. I asked if I could look around, and being a typically friendly Australian, the receptionist allowed me to do so. I was amazed at what I saw.

The atmosphere, the smell, the décor, the facilities – everything was wonderful. This was not what I expected to find in a care home. And, of course, the sun always shines in Perth, which helps too! I talked to a few residents who were all friendly and happy to chat to me, and all said how much they enjoyed living there.

As I have since learned, no one really wants to move into a care home unless they have to. They want to be in their own home if they have that choice available, which, of course, not everyone does have. But here was a group of people actually enjoying the experience.

While I recognise there are many establishments in our country providing excellent care, many are not. Seeing the care home in Perth brought home to me that the way we provided care here in the UK was falling short in some way, because for most people a care home is something to be avoided at all costs. In fact, in the intervening years since then, the trend to stay out of a care setting for as long as possible has become even more accentuated – not least because of the increasing costs of care, but also undeniably because care homes are, as a sector, perceived negatively.

And while it is perfectly sensible and desirable to want to remain independent in one's own home for as long as possible, people often leave it very late to make the move into care – so late, in fact, that by the time they do so, their health and quality of life can have become compromised through neglect, poor diet, or other factors such as isolation or accidents in the home.

Need it be that way – for a care home to be seen as the last option to be avoided for as long as possible? Why not make care homes so enjoyable and supportive that elderly people with the resources to do so move into them at the optimum point for them and their family, and enjoy the company and the peace of mind that really good care can provide?

I came away from the care setting in Perth thinking two things. One was, why can't all care in the UK be as good as that? And the second was, could I provide a care setting to match that and make a profit from doing so? I also had to ask myself if I was the right person to be going into a new field like this, as I had no direct experience of working with older people. But I did have a background that proved surprisingly relevant.

All through my career I had worked in an environment of looking after others in some way, including running a house for unaccompanied youngsters aged between sixteen and eighteen. Most of them were in no man's land: too old to be adopted or live in a children's home, but not yet old enough to look after themselves.

I had also set up and run HMOs (houses in multiple occupation) specifically for people living on benefits, including a number with alcohol or drug dependencies as well as individuals with mental health or disruptive behaviour issues, and some ex-offenders.

Both categories of accommodation require an element of care, because some of the residents are vulnerable in a number of ways, and both categories have a certain reputation for providing only the most basic of services. I felt that a different approach – adding value to the experience of being in accommodation like this – would reap dividends, and in both cases I was proven right.

I'd initially gone into this type of business because while I knew it meant extra work, an HMO will always deliver a better return than renting a property privately to a family, or even splitting it up into apartments.

At that point in my life I was time rich and money poor, and so was in a position to do all the management myself, from emptying the bins to collecting the rent. In return, I saw a 25%+ annual return on my capital instead of around 5%, and that set me on the road to building my property portfolio.

Throughout my time running HMOs I remained hands-on and personally involved. If I didn't want to go home one night, I would stay in one of my HMOs, which focused my mind on providing a setting that I myself would be happy to occupy day in, day out.

Above all, the HMOs showed me how delivering a better quality of service can really impact on return on investment (ROI). My HMOs were in London and Essex, and this was before the time when they had to be licensed. The quality of many HMOs locally was poor; with demand outstripping supply, owners knew they could get away with it.

I felt it could, and should, be done better. For instance, the contract I had with the council was to provide the residents in my HMOs with bed and breakfast for a standard charge – but my breakfast was a full English, not just cereal and toast. We also had a decent dining room, and as well as often making the breakfasts myself, I would eat there with the residents. And while there were no frills, the place was kept clean and tidy.

I got some thanks for it. In fact, people wanted to stay with me – sometimes for years – rather than move on to a B&B. Instead of residents regularly asking the council to find them somewhere else, which is what often happened with the other HMOs, they stayed put. That meant I took a lot of problems away from the council, so I was always top of their list to contact and my HMOs were always full.

Treating residents with respect encouraged them to treat their accommodation with respect. While there will always be incidents in settings like this, the amount of trouble I saw from residents was reduced, too. If there was someone acting out of order or becoming violent, the others would calm them down because they respected the place and took collective responsibility. Some of the residents even took it in turns to tend to the garden – not because I asked them to, but because they took an interest in it, and they knew they were staying long enough to enjoy it. Everyone benefited. We had less damage, too – when residents came home with no key, they thought, 'I like this place' and didn't kick the door in.

My HMOs were always full, profitable and relatively trouble free – and I still own a few today, although I'm not there to make the breakfasts any more.

I built up a small chain of HMOs, although that was far from easy because I didn't start off with a lot of capital. Lenders didn't recognise it as a business with a secure, regular income, so I bought properties needing a change of consent and refurbishment and did all the work myself, building up equity in that way, and re-mortgaging them. I was able to make the most of my capital and constantly reinvest it. But still it was a slow business: sometimes it took a year before I could acquire another HMO.

After a while I realised that I wanted to move into a sector where I could borrow and expand more easily, and that coincided with my 'Eureka' moment in Australia. Prior to my trip, I'd read some articles about managing care homes and attended some seminars, so this was on my radar. But visiting the home in Perth, and seeing how care homes could be run within the principles I would want to adopt and still be profitable, I realised it was feasible.

Developing the concept

I've often been asked, 'Did you start your care home from a business model or a care model perspective?'

Really it was a combination of the two, because the approach I took was to ask myself, 'Can I provide the experience and standards I want to provide and still make a profit?'

That was my starting point. I then asked, 'What does this picture of a quality, profitable care home look like?' I created the picture, the experience, the physical building on paper and I costed it down to the last pound. Then I looked at what income would be available for a care service like this. 'If I can't more than cover my costs,' I thought, 'then I don't start.'

It's fifteen years since I went around the care home in Australia, and the residents were much more able-bodied than those you would find in a typical care home today. In many ways, this has changed the type of care provided because most residents have to go into care homes rather than making this decision a positive lifestyle choice. Often, the decision is made in a hurry by relatives keen to get a loved one out of hospital following a fall or a sudden downturn in their health, or by the hospital looking to unblock a bed. The best homes are invariably full, and even run waiting lists. Because people are desperate to get into somewhere half decent, they then accept levels of service that they really shouldn't have to accept.

In addition, the pressure on many homes to provide rooms at local authority rates has added to the woes of the industry. The rates local authorities are prepared to pay are significantly below the cost of providing a quality service.

Inevitably, the 'bad apple' managers and staff who have been featured in the press have lowered the reputation of care homes, to the point where many older people, quite understandably, resist going in at all.

This situation not only serves older people poorly, it also reduces the business opportunities for good care home providers. If the quality of care and the environment were better throughout the system, many more people might well go into a care home earlier, as long as they could afford to. It wouldn't be seen as a retrograde last move, but more of a sideways step, or even an improvement on their current situation.

Far too many of those hanging on in their own homes are struggling to look after themselves (and sometimes their partner as well). They're only living in part of the house, finding it difficult and stressful to keep it maintained or even heated and ventilated properly. All too often, they are not cooking proper meals for themselves, and many go for days without seeing another person. This endangers their mental and physical wellbeing, and puts them particularly at risk from falls.

According to the National Institute for Health and Care Excellence (NICE), 'Falls are the leading cause of mortality resulting from injury in people aged seventy-five and older in the UK.'[1] The cost to

---

1   www.nice.org.uk/guidance/cg161/evidence/
     falls-full-guidance-190033741

society is also significant. According to the same report, falls and fractures in people aged sixty-five and over account for more than four million hospital bed days each year in England alone.

The strain that is put on family can be overwhelming, too, trying to visit from a distance and keep their loved one safe, warm and properly fed. Many carers end up poorly themselves, putting their relationships under pressure or having to give up work. They often feel they can never do enough and end up racked with guilt, as well as exhausted and possibly resentful too.

Imagine you're an older person going into a setting which is as good as your own home, plus it provides company, good food, warmth, security and care when you need it. That's the offer every care home should be making to the resident and to their family.

Every home that provides good quality care will almost certainly be able to tell you of residents who came in suffering from poor health and with a short life expectancy prognosis, only to recover and go on to live much longer than anyone had expected. I used to love it when new residents joined us, often having dreaded the move. Before long, they would be saying, 'I wasn't expecting it to be as nice as this' and 'Why didn't I do this earlier?' Often it wasn't a question of money that had kept them back; rather, they had dreaded the thought of a care home because of what they had read about them in the media, or examples of poor experiences they had heard from friends or relatives.

In many ways, the situation is similar to our hospitals today. People aren't paying their own bills, so they accept what they're given. The NHS is brilliant, but it's all delivered to a certain standard. And a lot of care homes are still like that, even when residents are paying top dollar. I put this down to the managers and staff who think, 'You need us so you're going to fit into the way we work – not the other way around.'

Care needn't and mustn't be delivered like that. And when it is, the responsibility for improving the situation must come from the top.

I couldn't live with myself if I provided a service like that.

And so the journey begins

When the trip around the care home in Perth opened my eyes to what was possible in a residential care facility for the elderly, I wondered if a model to that sort of standard could work in the UK.

I contacted the architect of the care home in Perth and we worked on some ideas and designs. He even came over to the UK and looked at a site I had in mind. Once I had done all my costings, I realised that my plans should be possible. I bought the site and, with the help of an English architect supported by ideas from the Australian architect, designed a new 64-bed care home: Silver Springs.

The site, at Thorrington in Essex, together with the construction represented a fair investment from scratch – around £4 million. Prior to this, I had put together all my business plans, working out what level of staffing I would require together with all the other costs. I came up with an average figure that we needed to charge: £650 per week on a 90% occupancy rate.

But could that be achieved?

I undertook some comparative analysis with various homes, and decided it could. In a worst-case scenario, I believed we could achieve an average of £600 per person, allowing for some local authority funded residents who would be paying considerably lower fees. With that and a 90% occupancy rate, we could deliver a great experience, cover all our costs, service our debts and still make a modest profit. A large part of me thought we could get much more than that – up to £900 per week – by delivering real excellence and making our home one that elderly people would want to live in. But all that lay in the future.

I looked at comparable care homes within quite a wide radius. Rightly or wrongly, I thought that the home would be so brilliant that people would come to it from a long way away. And quite a few did.

The business plan

So what was in my business plan? Following on from my discussions with the architect in Australia and my research here in the UK, I developed a (long) list of what we needed to include, which allowed me to do the costings. First, I looked at the 'critical mass' – the size of the home and the number of residents needed to make it viable – and came up with a figure of around sixty. That would be big enough to afford a wide range of facilities and resources, as well as provide an ongoing marketing budget, but still small enough for everyone in the home to get to know one another.

The rooms themselves needed to be significantly larger than those provided in the majority of homes at the time. We settled on 160ft^2 (15m^2) together with an en-suite bathroom/wet room and ample wardrobe and cupboard spaces as well as wide doors.

Moreover, I wanted all the rooms to have nice, big windows going down to the floor, or French windows on the ground floor, to provide lots of light as well as good views of the outside. And I made sure that every room looked out on to something interesting and pleasant. Each room had a big television, too. Yes, we could have made the rooms smaller and squeezed more in – but that was not what I wanted to do.

In terms of furnishing and decorating, we felt we needed to be open and flexible. With each new resident, we asked the same question: 'Your room is your home, how would you like it to be?' We did furnish some rooms with quality furniture and decorate them to be colour co-ordinated in a combination of cream, light blue and natural wood. This allowed people to see what could be provided, and some actually asked for that. Or each resident could bring their own furniture and choose their own colour scheme. From the outset, residents could feel that they had a say in their environment.

Now we needed to design in the activities that would keep them socially connected and mentally active.

The building was a U-shape, which proved practical in many ways, but a circle or a square would have served equally well. I might well experiment with one of those shapes with my next care home. There were three wings, one of which was for residents with dementia, each with approximately twenty residents' rooms. We named the dementia wing after my sister Caroline, who opened it for us. Each wing also had its own large lounge in a hexagonal shape – designed to let in as much light as possible – plus other smaller lounges in between the rooms. This meant no one had to walk far to go outside their own space to socialise, play cards and so on.

We had a large central room which we used for birthdays and social events, and we could bring in entertainers such as magicians. Today I would incorporate the facility for a mini cinema as the technology has moved on so much.

The outside of the building was important, too. While having plants, trees and other natural features was essential, I believed we could do much better than that by adding further features which would interest and entertain residents. Within the enclosed horseshoe, we created a children's play area for the benefit of visiting families, and so residents themselves could watch the children play. The playground idea came from Perth, where it was a hugely popular feature in the home I saw. One thing I learned from Australia was how important the family visits are to the residents, and I myself always took my children along when I visited my grandparents. But once visitors have had their cake and a cup of tea, the kids can get restless and start wrecking Granddad's glasses and so on. The playground feature certainly took the pressure off the visits for many of our residents.

We had chickens walking about and clucking away. They would come pecking at the doors sometimes, and we even gave residents bags of corn so they could feed the chickens if they wished. The chickens were something that came from my own background. I grew up with chickens; my father kept a few and I was always tasked with cleaning them out, which I thought was a right pain at the time. But they are such busy, colourful creatures, and many of the residents really loved to see and hear them.

We also had a lovely big dovecote for the same reason. Apart from being beautiful, birds provide such reassuring sounds of nature, as well as a talking point for the residents and visitors. I even used an image of doves as the symbol for the care home – which seemed very appropriate. We, like the dovecote, were providing a safe, secure place to live.

The chickens, the long windows, the playground, the doves – they were all designed to get people looking outwards, not inwards. And we added a pond, raised beds in the garden with flowers and vegetables, an aviary and greenhouse. All too often, care homes don't have a world outside to look at, just a fence or trees which can lead to the place feeling incredibly enclosed and cut off. I believe we managed to create a real alternative to that.

Inevitably, not all care homes can be in the country or on the edge of a town and enjoy pleasant views of nature, but even a busy road with people walking up and down can be used to the residents' advantage, providing a prospect that will help them feel connected and still part of life.

From the beginning, we planned to keep the residents busy and socially connected, and the extra rooms we set aside provided the space to help that happen. Regular clubs for playing cards and dominoes sprang up quickly, and we also set aside a room for arts and crafts which was popular too. Those residents who used it really appreciated it, and the people who ran the activities doubled up as carers so the staffing cost to us was minimal.

We also invested in our own minibus, taking residents on day trips to places like Clacton. This is not a cheap thing to do, but it represented a major selling point for those coming into the home who wanted to remain active. Some residents had family who could take them out for the day, but not all. We could fill that gap.

Our hair salon was a big hit as well. Two lovely young ladies came in and ran it as their own business, and we'd find all the 'customers' staying on long after they'd had their hair done to chat. It was a real morale booster for the residents – everyone likes to look at their best.

Takeaways

- Care must be tailored to the needs of the residents; the residents should not have to accommodate themselves to the needs of the managers and staff.

- The ideal care home needs to be big enough to be able to afford a wide variety of facilities and resources, but small enough for everyone in the home to get to know one another.

- It's important for residents to feel as if they have a say in their environment, choosing their own colour schemes if they wish to.

- An outward-looking layout with large windows overlooking gardens – ideally with animals and a playground for young visitors – helps residents to feel connected with the world beyond the home.

- Providing spaces for games and arts and crafts, and laying on minibus outings, encourages residents to stay active and maintain a positive outlook on life.

CHAPTER 2

Early Lessons Learned

Recruiting the right staff

Establishing a care home based on all the right values is only possible if you manage to recruit people who share your ideals of what good care looks like. And that's where I learned a lot in a very short space of time.

Originally my preference was to design and build the home and appoint a manager to deliver the promise I wanted. However, very early on, I came unstuck. I just couldn't find someone to share my vision. So much so that I moved in myself for 18 months to make it work. Perhaps it was my naivety or lack of experience in this specific field, but I was surprised at the disconnect between what I had envisioned as the ethos of the home and the approach of some of the people I initially appointed.

Only 60% of those I first recruited matched my expectations – which meant that 40% didn't. This didn't make them bad carers, please don't get me wrong. Arguably, my care home just wasn't right for them. But to me it seemed – rightly or wrongly – that for some of the people who came to work for me, it was just a job. I wanted people with deep down caring; staff with the right values and attitude, who would always put the residents first.

Of the staff who I felt weren't relating to our residents as I wanted, I managed to get some back on track with additional training, but some were just never going to fit in with my ethos. It took a while before I found the person to run my home the way I wanted it run.

Early on, I remember overhearing a carer in conversation with a resident, telling them they couldn't have an extra dessert. It was totally against everything I'd ever thought and tried to instil in my staff. I then looked at myself and wondered if it was my fault that the member of staff had taken that approach. That was a wake-up call for me; I'd given all my staff an overview of the sort of care I wanted to provide, but if I hadn't told them specifically about details like that, their default response would have been ideas and cultures from other homes they'd worked in. I had to go back and talk to them collectively about the attention to detail that defined the service I was after.

Looking back, I have to blame myself for this disconnect. There's an old saying that 'the fish stinks from the head down'. I was in charge and so it was down to me to make clear what I expected right from the start. Change had to come from the top.

I introduced another part to the induction sessions in addition to the carer training (which I also delivered myself) from the values point of view. After a couple of days, anyone can become a carer and get a certificate, but actually there's a hell of a lot more to it than that. I worked through a long list of considerations, from how carers address residents to asking them when they wished to have their curtains opened in the morning. Everyone likes things done differently, and carers need to respond to that.

This list formed the operating manual that I developed and refined for every aspect of the running of the care home. This systematic approach (which I talk about in much more detail later in the book) helped define exactly what everyone was expected to do, and the majority of personnel found this helpful as it made their lives much more straightforward.

For those who entered into the spirit, I believe it positively affected their work experience. I was often told at the time – and have been since – that it helped staff enjoy their work more, and brought them closer to the residents themselves. They often spent a lot more time with a resident than they would have done in a usual practice, but I had built that into my plans by having higher staff-to-resident ratios than normally found in a care home. It helped when we experienced the regular problem faced by every care home – when several staff are tied up handling a major problem with one resident and the call bell rings from other residents who have needs to be met.

Eventually, I looked for different ways of sourcing the people I wanted and started recruiting from outside the care sector, including the hospitality industry, hoping to attract those well used to working hard to win and retain customers who could vote with their feet. I even used differently worded ads and placed them in different parts of the newspaper, presenting my business as 'not your standard care home' but more of a hotel. I took on youngsters straight out of school; I knew that the practical aspects of caring could be easily taught as long as we had the right human raw material. I made it worthwhile for the right people to work for me by paying a touch more than my competitors to attract the cream of the local caring community.

What does deep down caring look like? For me, residents need to be engaged in the conversation and asked, 'How can we make your stay with us the very best it can be?' And that extends to respecting individual wishes – not taking it for granted that residents all want to eat at a certain time, or get up in the morning at the time best suited to the staff rota. There's only a small part of the experience that all care homes have to insist happens in a certain way: the nursing and medication element. But we've got no right to dictate to residents about the rest of the service they receive. This is their life, their home.

So, our staff didn't tell residents what they had to have. We asked them what they wanted and did our best to provide that. Yes, we had a routine which many people liked and found reassuring, but it wasn't fixed in stone. Plenty of our residents personally set the template for the services we provided for them.

Marketing the new care home

As every care home operator will appreciate, the main concern I had before I opened was whether I would be able to attract enough residents – especially at the outset when I had not established my reputation. Success early on can be heavily reliant on good marketing.

We started marketing with a local company and agreed a strategy, a large part of which was to have the home opened by a personality, and we got hold of Angela Rippon. She was perfect for it: very professional and excellent with the media (as you would expect), and the day turned out superbly with lots of attendant press coverage. We also sent out flyers, placed ads in the local paper and worked hard on the PR. But curiously, when we checked back to see how people had come across us, many mentioned seeing the large sign we had put up in front of the home. That just goes to show that sometimes, the simple and most obvious things can have the biggest effect.

While I got a lot of things right, much has changed in the years since I opened Silver Springs, and my knowledge of marketing has expanded significantly. In Chapter 4 I emphasise its importance for every care home, and set out how I would now approach the challenge. In total, I spent over £30,000 on launching the home, which might seem a lot, but marketing should never be seen as an expense but as an investment, as long as you can quantify and justify the return on that investment.

Despite my initial concerns, and (at least in part) because of our marketing efforts, the home started to fill quickly. Getting the first few residents to come into a new care home will always be a challenge, simply because there's no one else living there to ask how good it is. But we needn't have worried as there was obviously a latent demand locally.

What really shocked me, however, was that we immediately had an injection of twenty people from other homes who were not happy with the care they were receiving. That probably didn't make me very popular with the homes they had come from, but I had no sympathy when I learned why people had wanted to leave.

There have, in fairness, been several better homes built since in the locality, but I caught the market at just the right time.

Problems to be solved

In my introduction, I said that I had seen my share of setbacks in business along the way, but that these presented learning opportunities. This was certainly the case with the care home.

To be honest, I was somewhat scared of the care side of things. But it isn't just about care, it's about hospitality, too – looking after people. I was largely happy with some of the key aspects for which I had been responsible – the design of the care home, size of rooms and windows, and, not least, the chickens! However, some of the staff let me know that they felt they weren't being treated properly. Their big beef – leading to the single change that made the biggest difference to the way they felt about their work – was the shift rotas, which had not been designed in consultation with them.

It sounds obvious, but working nights will suit some people and not others. So why would anyone tell people which shifts they must work when managers get a much better solution if they just ask staff what their preferences are? I found out who wanted which shifts, and decided that no one should have to work nights if they didn't want to. This helped staff morale, and helped in future recruitment as well, because we could advertise for shifts that really fitted in with people who wanted to work days, nights, weekends, and so on. We only needed six people on at night, compared to eighteen on days, so that meant recruiting just eight people to allow for holidays and absences. We applied a four-week rolling rota so staff could book holidays and medical and dental appointments, and have a little swap around between themselves if they ever wanted to. We even thought about having a crèche to help those with childcare responsibilities.

Sorting out the rotas proved really important. I saw how it shouldn't be done, often leading to people leaving – and it's usually the good ones who go when things aren't right, because they can. It represented a watershed – working with our staff to meet their needs as far as possible as well as our own.

We were helped by having a number of staff who were happy to live on site. A handful of overseas staff lived in a bungalow next to the care home – so every now and again when we had a staff shortage, they could fill in the gap for us. I would always recommend designing in that sort of flexibility. Care homes often use agencies to fill staff shortages; that's not only expensive, but also you never know who is going to turn up or whether they will fit into your way of working. Effectively, we had our own agency on site. There were obviously rules and regulations around how many hours the onsite staff could work, but only once in a blue moon did we ever need to call on an outside agency.

We also allowed staff to work double shifts as long as they had a proper break in between, and we provided their food too – which seems an obvious thing to do as care homes normally have food left over. Providing meals represents such a small cost to the home, but reaps big dividends as a way of rewarding staff. It saved our personnel money as well as time at home, and they were appreciative.

We had a nurse on board doing night shifts, although we didn't technically require one to begin with as we weren't a registered nursing home. But I provided one anyway, and all within the budget, even though she was earning well over the hourly rate of the other staff. She was invaluable, a real rock, and brought a different dimension to the care we could provide.

The importance of the kitchen

Right from the start, a lot of emphasis – and resources – went into making the food and dining experience of our residents as good as it could possibly be. When people reach the latter stage of their lives, food is often one of their chief pleasures. Making the business of sitting down to a meal with fellow residents something they look forward to is really important – a social highlight of each day, just as it is in many families. I've been heartened over recent years to see a few care homes actually appointing top chefs – making it a big selling point for their homes, and focusing on providing attractive, nutritious food that residents not only enjoy, but also find easy to eat. Looking back, though, we were certainly ahead of that trend in our approach to the dining experience of our residents.

Our kitchen was designed like that of a busy restaurant, with the work going on in full view of the diners. This was quite deliberate; I thought that part of the dining experience should involve the residents being in close proximity to the bustle and aromas of the kitchen, especially breakfast cooking in the morning and the afternoon cakes. This was their home, after all, and what smells and tastes more like home than home baking? We had to put in place the equipment to cope with sixty-four plus people – sometimes, as at Christmas, all wanting to eat at once. With guests, we often passed the ninety mark.

A priority from the beginning was to employ a proper chef, not just a good cook. And while that meant paying a higher salary, we really got our money's worth. A properly trained chef will know how to run a kitchen efficiently and organise the staff, order food and not waste it. I could get into a kitchen myself and cook a meal, and did so on a number of occasions, but a chef knows how to design nutritious and well-balanced menus, get tomorrow's meals prepared, and so on. What you pay them above and beyond what you'd pay a competent cook, you get back in higher quality, better management and reduced waste.

Having a trained chef was also important because we always had a number of people with specific dietary requirements. And while in a care home setting you have the luxury of knowing in advance how many people you are cooking for in total, it still takes imagination and often some spontaneity to offer appetising meals consistently for people with many different requirements.

Choice is seriously important. After all, those of us not living in a care home can choose whatever we're going to eat every day, so why should care home residents be any different? We would always have three choices for each course at each mealtime. At breakfast, a full English was always available, plus the special of the day – bubble and squeak, for instance, kippers or smoked haddock – plus porridge and cereals. But if residents wanted to have kippers every day, they only had to ask. The only caveat we applied was that their choices must comply with their dietary requirements.

At every mealtime, they could order at the table rather than hours in advance, allowing them the option to change their minds, and a carer would get their meals for them, making sure they received as much or as little as they liked of each item. That level of portion control minimised waste and ensured that no one was faced with too much food on their plate, or vegetables they didn't want. We were particularly careful about the meats we served because some can be chewy, but fish was always popular, especially fish pie. We had mashed potato as an option with every meal – even on Fridays when fish and chips were on the menu – because some residents found that easier to get on with. We had plenty of vegetables to choose from, too, because they are a vital source of vitamins and fibre, which older people especially need, so care homes can't stint on them.

Nutrition is as vital a part of the care package as anything else. Being the sole provider of nutrition for a vulnerable older person is a huge responsibility.

But the key to achieving a balanced diet, for me, was providing food that the residents found appetising as well as easy to eat.

While desserts may not have been nutritionally so important, the sweet trolley was seen as a real treat. It was not only hugely popular, but helped to keep the calorie intake up where residents needed it, so we always had a good choice of the old favourites.

Yes, we had some food left over because of the choices we offered, but staff meals absorbed a lot of that – another good reason to provide them – and our chef was often able to recycle ingredients.

Above all, each meal was treated as a social occasion. We had seven residents round each table, and people would spend up to several hours there. It was a get-together as much as a meal – a chance to chat.

Having quality cutlery, tableware and linen tablecloths was important, too – again adding to the feeling that the residents were in a good hotel or back at home. Of course, there is extra effort involved in keeping everything nice, but it's worth that effort. I conducted regular surveys, asking residents what meals they were enjoying, what their favourite foods were, and got some excellent feedback. I then made sure we included the residents' favourites in the menu now and again.

Inevitably, there were personality conflicts sometimes at the tables. We always had a few struggling with their food or making a bit of a noise, but that's par for the course and we got used to it, and so did the other residents – who were usually patient. Incontinence was something we had to deal with as well. One way we reduced the problem was to design in three toilets very close to the dining room – important because older people sometimes can't wait and will often take a long time.

There can come a point where some residents will prefer to eat in their own room, although that deprives them of an important focal point of their day. Of those who preferred to eat in their rooms, they did this partly through care needs and partly through shyness, while some people simply preferred their own company. Because someone is old doesn't mean to say they're more confident. In fact, they're often more sensitive and potentially more easily embarrassed. But sometimes shyness can be overcome.

When the father of a personal friend came to live with us, he didn't even want to be in a care home, let alone come to meals. He preferred to sit and watch TV in his room. One day we managed to get him down to have his hair cut in our salon, and then suggested that he might have dinner with us, and he did. And he came down every day after that. He just needed a little help breaking the ice.

Getting on an even keel

I recognised early on that I was at the beginning of a large learning curve, with plenty that I could improve upon in the home. In fact, I'd go as far as to say I became consumed by it and actually moved in. The dynamics or chemistry of the place wasn't quite right, and working out what mattered most to the residents enabled me to recognise where the shortcomings were.

Because we initially parted company with two managers in quick succession, the council actually put a temporary embargo on the home. Looking back, I wonder how we must have appeared from the outside and I can appreciate why the council did that. A care home has to be run by someone with a background in care.

I had several meetings with both the local authority and the Care Quality Commission (CQC) and found them very supportive when I explained exactly what I was looking to achieve. I would always suggest getting in touch with these authorities for direct advice rather than second guessing what they might be expecting, or hiring experts to act as intermediaries.

I was disappointed to lose time in getting the home to the level I'd been looking for. I was naïve and probably didn't really know what qualities I was looking for in a manager, so responsibility was certainly in part mine. I did find someone in the end – a lovely lady who more than fitted the bill – and she played a huge part in the success we enjoyed. After we got Silver Springs running smoothly, she was always saying to me, 'Can't we do another one?'

What were her attributes? With her it was always residents first, whatever it takes. She was naturally caring and she had previously run her own homes, so she had a business perspective as well as knowing how to deliver resident care. But I didn't need her for her business skills, to be honest. In my original budgets, I had two managers – the care manager and the business manager – and I became the business manager, which was straightforward for me.

Next time, I would actually appoint three managers: one responsible for care, one for hospitality and one to run the business. Even if a care manager can do the other sides of things, it takes up their time and attention. I want my care manager to be out walking round the home as often as possible, talking to people, watching what's going on, not doing paperwork.

With the new manager in place, the home went from strength to strength and rapidly filled up, and although we did take in some local authority placements in the beginning, we reached an average of £700 per week per person inside the first year, and then went on to £850 in the second year. With costs remaining inside our original budgets and the home at or close to capacity, it was now making a very healthy return. While we did maintain a good marketing spend to ensure we remained full, most of our vacancies were being taken up through recommendations.

A bare two years after Silver Springs opened, I reached the point where I couldn't refine what I had any further, or add any more value to the home – and Care UK made an offer that I felt unable to refuse. My investment had almost doubled in a very short space of time. At that point, one of my first thoughts was to replicate what I had achieved in another part of the country, but I was diverted by other opportunities that came my way.

However, that ambition still burns inside me, and now I know exactly what to do from day one. I have the business template and the care model all in place and the land to make it happen.

Watch this space.

Takeaways

- Recruiting staff who always put the residents first is crucial if you are to run a care home that reflects caring values.

- Recruiting through a range of channels, including from outside the care sector, will enable you to select staff with the right attitudes.

- A focus on the hospitality side of the business will ensure that the concept of 'looking after people' is top of the agenda.

- Accommodating preferences for working patterns will contribute to staff retention and foster a contented and co-operative workforce.

- Mealtimes that offer choice, the company of fellow residents, and nutritious food designed to cater for their needs are vital for wellbeing.

- A committed care manager focused on the resident experience is vital for the success of any care home.

CHAPTER 3

Establishing The Promise

I n the following sections, I set out the key areas which I believe a prospective care home owner needs to address in order to achieve great care – and a handsome return for their capital. And to me, that means establishing the promise and then delivering it.

So first off, what do I mean by the promise in a care setting?

What makes a great care home?

Great care should be available to everyone. It's not a pipe dream. It is doable, and it should be affordable.

It might sound odd, but excellent care was not number one or even number two on my list of what I needed to provide when I set out my first plans. Excellent care was a given, a need which residents should expect to be met. I wanted to go one step further and create a care home model focused on the aspirations of its residents.

The foundation of every care home should be the promise it makes, primarily to residents, but also to staff, investors, other stakeholders and so on. That promise is the customer experience it is committed to delivering. It not only sets the tone for how the home is designed and equipped and the way staff approach their work, it also becomes the platform for your marketing and sales efforts. I know this sounds obvious, but it's all too easy to start planning your marketing when you haven't yet clarified what it is you are promising potential residents and their families.

Sitting down and analysing what it is you want to offer can crystallise your business plan, helping you with important aspects such as borrowing or raising capital. What sets you apart? What experience will you be offering that perhaps is not available elsewhere and that will help you win and retain business?

The promise comes right at the outset. And then of course you need to deliver what you have promised, because failure to do so means unfulfilled expectations which can be hugely damaging for a business. You don't want to overpromise and underperform in this of all sectors.

When I worked on developing the promise for my care home, my starting point was my parents. I thought, 'I'm going to build a home that I would happily see my mum and dad living in. What does it need to look like?'

Of course, when the home is open and you're having to deliver on your promises, everything has to be properly organised and systemised. I did that by bringing together a series of SOPs – standard operating procedures – on every aspect of running the home which combined to form a comprehensive manual. Staff read that when they joined so every member of personnel knew what their role required and could see how they fitted into the total picture.

When I developed the promise for Silver Springs, I had my father especially in my mind. What would his concerns, wishes and hopes be if he was moving out of his own home and into care? If I could make him happy, I knew I could make it work for most other people, too. He actually did go and look at the home after we'd built it and fortunately he liked what he saw, although he didn't feel that the time was right for him to move in!

What do families look for?

Using my dad as my target audience wasn't a bad angle as it's usually the sons and daughters who make the choice of care home on behalf of their parents. Working out what those relatives would base their decisions on became another of my obsessions. I took notes of our original conversations when they came to look at the care home, and talked to them again when I'd got to know them after their loved one had settled in.

Their overriding concern will always be, 'Will this home look after my mum or dad properly?' but a host of other factors can come into play – not least convenience and cost.

Humans are all open to persuasion by our initial responses. We don't get a second chance to make a good first impression. One of the key factors for prospective residents and their families turned out to be how the home smelt. The right temperature, nice lighting and so on were important, but the smell of a place is often what hits people first and remains with them.

Of course, every care home has a potential problem here – one that I dealt with in a practical way. We had an hourly air changing system installed throughout the home, which had the important additional benefit of reducing the spread of infections. Aromatherapy operates in many businesses, not least the retail and hospitality sectors; it is a mood changer and creator. What care homes mustn't do is cover up bad smells with good smells by means of aerosols and other devices. If homes try to mask the problem and don't sort out the bad smells, they become an unhealthy and unpleasant cocktail.

We didn't have overcooked cabbage lingering in the air either – one of the odours commonly associated with a nursing home. Instead we had lovely cooking smells wafting through part of the home as we deliberately designed the kitchens to be open for the residents to see and smell. They could see the chef running around, so it looked, felt and smelt like home. We could close the hatch when needed – for fire safety and when clearing up at the end of a meal, as this could be quite noisy.

So we accentuated the good smells and took action on the not-so-good ones. And we did that by using the best chemicals and having separate, fully-equipped cleaning cupboards strategically dotted around the home. That way staff weren't trailing cleaning equipment around and could deal with an accident quickly and efficiently.

We also had a separate team of cleaning staff whose priority was tackling spills promptly and thoroughly. Accidents happen, and many residents are in a care home because they have continence issues, which makes it vital for staff to act quickly, thoroughly and respectfully.

We didn't go down the polished floor route, which would have made it easier to deal with spills, but doesn't make for a lovely environment. We had carpets in the hallways and in every room where the residents wanted them – although we did fit stain- and water-resistant ones.

What else do families look for? That all-important first visit can prove make or break, and we liked to show our home off at its best. We often got people to visit during afternoon tea – where they could see the residents enjoying a proper tea with lovely china, like the Ritz, and tantalising baking smells coming from the kitchen. But I always invited visitors to see every other aspect of the home, too – not just the birds, children's area and fountains, but the kitchens and laundry, so they knew how we worked.

A family member who is keen to make sure that a home isn't simply putting on appearances will visit unannounced. To me that's quite right – and I'm sure they will make allowances if they arrive just as you are getting residents up in the morning and everyone is in a rush!

Getting the ratios right

Staff-to-resident ratios will always be important to families and residents, along with the calibre of those employed by a care home. We deliberately took on higher numbers than industry standards, as well as taking a flexible approach to how we made use of them during the busiest times. It only takes one or two additional people to make a positive difference, and the reverse is true: being one or two down on a shift can really cause issues.

Many care homes run such tight ships that they leave themselves vulnerable if someone doesn't turn up for their shift or someone leaves and can't be replaced quickly. We had the flexibility of effectively having a bank of our own staff living on site, but we also had floating staff between the wings, so that if a resident needed additional attention, as so often happens, we could cope with that.

The manager always made herself available at key times and turned her hand to whatever was needed, and the staff we took on to handle entertainment and activities were also carers. Inevitably there were times when everyone was flat out, especially if more than one person needed extra attention, but such times were very much the exception.

Having enough staff leads to a calmer atmosphere in the home, and you don't get good people leaving because they feel constantly under pressure and unable to provide good quality care.

The legal requirement of staffing levels is 'adequate'. Wages are the biggest single expense, and the temptation for anyone keen to keep costs tight is to run rotas that leave little room for manoeuvre if things go wrong. The staff-to-residents ratio is one of the critical factors every home has to get right to ensure they are not caught out when a staff member doesn't turn up or a resident needs additional care. This makes staffing levels a vital ingredient to cost out properly for anyone planning to set up a care home.

Staff are a vital part of the promise

An important part of our promise to prospective residents was based on having higher than adequate staffing levels, and our residents responded

CARE

positively to having the same staff regularly looking after them. It is a very personal, even intimate
relationship; you cannot achieve that consistency using agency staff. So it's important to think
through ways of not relying on agency staff.

In addition, we assigned each resident their own
personal key worker who would be responsible for
maintaining their care plan, and be known to the
resident's family. That worked really well for us
and for the residents; it also gave staff a sense of
ownership and personal responsibility. As someone's key worker, the staff member is their friend,
their champion, their advocate – looking out for
them and going the extra mile to make sure they
get the service they need from all the other members of staff. This can be especially valuable for
those residents who either cannot articulate their
needs well or are shy about asking for extra help
or attention when necessary. Key workers became
the go-to person for each individual resident.

That became a big part of the promise we made to
new residents and their families: 'This is the person
you can rely upon to know exactly how your mum
or dad is feeling every day.'

54

Good record keeping

Of course, everyone in a home needs to know how an individual is faring, not least the care manager. And that relies upon sharing information, possibly with the local GP practice too.

One of the areas which I would now change radically from how we did it at Silver Springs is the way we kept notes on residents. Then it was all paper based; now there are some great cloud-based systems available which not only ensure the job is done properly, but also that everyone who needs access to the information on an individual's personal care plan and health notes can log in and get up to speed at any time.

Good record keeping was a challenge to us then, but now that so many more residents have complex health issues, it has become even more vital. The challenge is to run your home every day as if an inspection could be happening that day.

Personalised hospitality plans

While the care plan has to be agreed with the resident and their family, so too should their personalised hospitality plan.

The question to ask is, 'As well as your needs, what are your wants – your aspirations?' For example, 'How and when do you want to be woken up in the morning?'

It should definitely not be a matter of 'Breakfast is at half seven to nine, try not to miss it.' That's nonsense. Ask, 'How, when, where would you like breakfast and what would you like to eat?'

It is also important to bear in mind that some people are shy about coming to communal activities such as meals and social events, and can even be anxious about going to the hair salon, especially if they have a condition they are concerned about. That's why it's so important to discuss these details early on when a resident comes into a care home to determine their wishes and preferences, answer any concerns and give them all their options.

The laundry matters

Small details such as how you will look after their laundry matter when you make your promise to a resident. They've spent their life as a proud individual, looking after themselves and probably others as well, and now they're handing over responsibility and control for such a personal part of their life. Of course, the details are important and should be handled sensitively and with respect.

Many people will be keen to keep looking their best – and you can help them achieve that. Discussing their preferences early on, such as how they would like each of the items in their wardrobe to be cleaned, can settle their concerns, make them feel at home and maintain their dignity.

Conversely, one of the most depressing, demeaning and all-too-common things that can happen in a care home is for someone to end up with another person's clothes. It is really upsetting for the family to come in and see their loved one dressed in the wrong dress or jumper, or an item they have bought for a loved one being worn by somebody else. Tagging clothes properly – including using barcodes to avoid having large, ugly labels – solves that problem, as long as staff are sufficiently careful and vigilant.

We didn't have carers putting clothing in laundry baskets; we had our cleaners – the wonderful 'Pink Ladies' who turned out to be real treasures – doing it. Because they were so chatty, they got to know the wishes and the clothes of the residents and would put their items in personal baskets in their room. They also acted quickly and discreetly when accidents occurred.

Furniture and fittings

Moving out of their own home into the relative confines of a care setting can be quite traumatic for an elderly person – just as it would be for someone of any age. But it has particular importance as it will inevitably be seen as a last move and mean sacrificing so much of the space and independence they've enjoyed before. One of the most obvious ways to smooth that transition is by giving each resident carte blanche on their furniture and décor, including incorporating their own items if they wish.

We encouraged our residents to choose exactly how they wanted their room to be, and what they wanted to retain from their old life. That could sometimes mean making some unusual compromises.

One resident, a lovely old lady, came in with a great many boxes, which she had filled with all the memorabilia of her life. She was keen to keep all those memories, and who were we to deny her? So, we installed additional shelving. It reminded me of my nan's home: boxes everywhere. The lady was surrounded by her boxes containing all the things that mattered most to her until the day she died – and she loved it just the way it was.

It was probably my favourite resident's room.

Catering for all tastes

I've already talked about the importance of the kitchen in Chapter 2, and certainly near the top of the must-have list for prospective residents will be good quality food, with plenty of choice. When I imagined the ideal home for my dad, good food was right in at number one. That's why I employed a highly competent chef.

A chef is an investment that will help sell the home to people. From a business management perspective, they will know all about minimising wastage and getting the most out of their staff. They are the nucleus of a home, and all you will save by getting in a second-rate chef is a few thousand pounds.

A care home's kitchen can be operating for anything up to eighty hours a week – especially when it's offering the sort of flexibility we did. So, if your chef isn't on duty, they need an able number two, trained to provide food that they've designed. And hopefully a number three behind him/her as well with homes of a certain size. In terms of your home delivering quality food and a responsive service, the residents should never be able to tell when the main chef is absent – the chef is only as good as what happens on their day off.

Enabling couples to remain together

Keeping couples together is essential – why should partners be separated during their last years? But I do feel this is one facility that not enough care providers offer, presumably because it is not convenient to organise in some homes. However, the advantages of enabling partners to remain together, even as the health of one deteriorates, are considerable.

The 'village' model of care (where the elderly can move about the village from independent living through to supported living, and on to a care home) represents an ideal option in many ways, allowing people to continue to live in the same place as their care needs change. This model keeps couples together as far as possible, and they have nursing and domiciliary care on hand when needed. There are some excellent models now in this country.

Quite apart from the potential to keep partners together, the village model of care provides enormous reassurance for anyone coming in at whatever stage of their life (or that of their partner) through knowing that they can continue to live close to the other residents who come to form an important part of their social network. I believe this will help developments to entice more able older people in at an earlier point in their lives.

Certainly my next venture in the care field will provide reassurance to prospective residents that they can remain in their chosen home for as long as they need.

Local consultation

One of the hurdles any prospective care home owner faces is getting planning consent. While authorities will not usually be averse to more care resources in their locality, not every local resident will be pleased to have a large new development on their doorstep, especially if it impacts on their view or amenities.

There is also another important consideration for every prospective developer (and their financial backers) – just how much take up will there be for the new care home?

Both these issues can be resolved with sensible and transparent local consultation. At as early a stage as you can do so, engage local people in a meaningful consultation process. This will not only make sure you tick all the right boxes with the planners (and so head off objections at the pass), if managed properly, it can also provide interesting and helpful data in terms of future demand and what local people would like to have available in the vicinity.

Talking openly, being seen to take on board people's concerns, ideas and suggestions on everything from design to how the home can contribute to the local community in terms of providing a hub for activities, and how many jobs it will create, you will lead to a development that will be half way towards being full from day one – and will have the support of the local community. Don't take a design that seems to be fixed in stone along to engagement events at the pre-application stage; instead, offer up outline ideas and alternatives, and emphasise that you want to listen to constructive input and suggestions. Then, throughout the application process, engage local people at each stage, keeping them informed, listening to input and letting them know when ideas or concerns have been taken on board.

And while there will always be those who will object on principle to any form of development, you can reach out to others in the community – such as older people's groups and forums – who will see it as being in their best interests for new accommodation to be built locally. Usually these types of people will be keen to provide constructive input towards the creation of what may well prove to be their own home in years to come.

The objection that is often raised in communities when older people's housing or a care facility is proposed is that the biggest priority locally is new affordable housing for young people, and any available land should go in that direction. The counter-argument is often forgotten: every time an elderly person moves out of their existing home, they make that home available to a local family. Moreover, having care facilities locally enables elderly people to remain close to their existing friends, family and support networks and 'age in place'. So often people are forced to move miles away from their neighbourhood to get the care they need.

A good care facility can be a major contribution to the local community – especially if that community feels engaged with it from the start.

Takeaways

- Set out what you plan to provide in terms of care, service and resident experience before you open your doors. This will be your promise.

- Staff will play a key role in delivering the detail of that promise – make sure they know what's expected of them.

- Sensible staff ratios are critical if you are to deliver good care and not overstress your employees.

- You don't get a second chance to make a good first impression. Think about the ambience, lighting and smell of your home when a person first walks in.

- Choice really matters. Build each resident's stay in your home around their individual care and hospitality plan.

CHAPTER 4

Promoting The Promise

Marketing and sales

A strategic continuing marketing plan should form a crucial role in ensuring that a care home is kept full and therefore profitable. And yet few care homes outside of the larger groups seem to put consistent effort into this.

We ran a relatively successful campaign to keep the name of our home in front of people – not just while we were still establishing our reputation; we continued working at it even when the home filled up. Why is that continuity so important? Because in this sector it can sometimes take a long time for a lead to convert into a sale, and there will always be a turnover of places to fill. It's also the last few places being filled in a care home that provide the icing on the cake in terms of profit.

Ultimately a good home will always win new business by word of mouth, but this will still need to be supported by a quality sustained marketing and sales effort – especially if you have a lot of local competition.

In the years since I opened my home in Essex, marketing has moved on light years, partly because digital techniques have now become so powerful, but also because there are some great CRM (customer relationship management) software programs available to ensure you are making every pound you spend work hard. I would now employ similar tactics to promote a care home to those I use in successfully promoting my other businesses – including my wedding venues. For my wedding hotels, I know that we only achieve profitability once we reach a certain capacity across five separate venues, and every sinew is strained each month to ensure we reach and surpass that mark.

Some basic principles have not changed since I opened my care home: you still need to generate leads through marketing and then convert as many as possible through your sales operation, but the way you generate those leads has changed fundamentally.

Step 1: Generate leads

I look upon leads like fish: you need to throw bait out onto the water on a regular basis to get those fish interested in biting. For me, PR has always been an excellent way to achieve this – getting the public interested in your product when they read positive things about you in the media. But what generally happens now when someone reads about you? They go straight to your website to check you out.

When they get there, they don't just need to be reassured about your philosophy and facilities. They would also ideally like to learn something which will make their decision-making process easier: independently written, helpful, useful information on care in later life that tells them that you know what you're talking about and are keen to help anyone looking to make an important choice.

This is classic content marketing, proven to pay dividends. Give something of value to people who visit your website rather than simply try and sell them something, and you then open up a different sort of relationship where they will listen to you more readily. Help them to conclude that you are a professional and you're friendly, knowledgeable and helpful. When they come to a purchasing decision (which might be at any time in the future) you'll be on their short list.

Good content on a website, combined with canny search engine optimisation, will help drive traffic to your site from anybody looking online for a care home in your area. Google will give precedence to the sites with original, helpful content (especially if you can encourage other websites to have links to yours). Appear on the first page in a Google search and you are half way to generating a new lead out of the blue.

Of course, traditional forms of marketing can be critical too: advertising in local media, producing helpful brochures to respond to leads (not everyone is online), and supporting and sponsoring local causes or older people's groups.

Step 2: Work your database

Generating leads can be hard and sometimes costly work, so maximising the value of every single enquiry is essential. That means harnessing every lead that comes your way, categorising it (hot, warm, cool, immediate, long-term and so on) and then keeping in touch with that database on a regular (but not annoying) basis.

Sending a steady flow of interesting newsletters (digital or hard copy), inviting people to open days and events and so on, will keep your leads warm. They can always unsubscribe if they wish. Again, information which assists and informs people rather than simply extolling the virtues of your care home will be seen as far more valuable, and so retained and appreciated.

Putting residents' relatives on the circulation list will have the additional benefit of keeping them informed of what's happening at the home, which can be very reassuring.

The helpful content in the newsletters can be in the form of blogs, comment pieces, market information or news posts which are housed on your website, perhaps with links to reports or studies. All of this can drive traffic there, especially if you also use social media to draw attention to the posts.

Facebook and Twitter are excellent at keeping your name out there and developing followers, but leads through social media do need to be regularly followed up.

If all this sounds like hard work, well, it is, although modern CRM systems have taken a lot of the slog out of it. But when every converted lead, assuming a resident comes to stay for two years, brings around £60,000 to your business, it's certainly worth the effort.

Critically, the care home owner or manager needs to get marketing functioning in a way that isn't done 'when I get time' or constantly interrupted by them keeping the business running. Equally the task shouldn't be passed to someone who either has no time or lacks the seniority or knowledge to speak for you – which is what marketing is, after all. Yet all too often, this important part of the business is left to someone fairly junior, or the manager themselves tries to squeeze it in between other tasks, but then finds day-to-day pressures taking priority.

It can prove far better to employ someone from inside or outside the company who knows what they are doing. Marketing should not be seen as a 'nice to have' or 'costly extra'. It is an investment in the future of the business. And most definitely it should not be relegated to the 'must get around to that' category in the care manager's to-do list.

Investing in quality will always pay dividends, too. Mediocre photographs taken on your smartphone will never have the same impact as a well shot professional photograph. Moreover, if you use a photographer properly, you can get a series of shots taken in the space of a few hours that can be used and reused in the future. Local newspapers, for instance, can often be persuaded to run a story if there's a good photograph with people in it, and the same image can go into your website, newsletter and sales collateral.

To me a marketing budget is derived from answering the question: how much is a new customer worth? If you spend £1 and generate £2 in profit as a direct result, then your budget is potentially infinite. But to make sure you actually know that your investment is paying off, rigorous analysis should be part of the process. Just knowing that you've generated ten leads from your monthly marketing effort is not enough. Neither is knowing that a specific activity generates a certain number of leads. Every lead needs to be tagged and followed through the system, so you know what has generated it, when it sparks a viewing, then a conversion, and you can tell which form of marketing has generated the most valuable leads. That's your vein of gold – and once you establish what works best for you, keep using those methods.

Some marketing activities aren't just about generating a set number of leads in a month. Some are about forming and maintaining relationships, and social media falls firmly into that category. Assessing which form of social media works best for you is critical. There are lots to choose from, some being more relevant than others, but the right ones really can pay dividends. But they only produce the goods if you work at them consistently, ensure that you stay on message and continue to use them as a way of keeping in touch with your various audiences and reinforcing your values and ethos.

Twitter, for instance, can build relationships with others in your sector and in relevant local organisations – people who can easily influence your potential customers. Twitter allows you to comment (briefly) on key issues in the care sector, and so demonstrate your ethos and thought leadership, to share useful news, comment positively on or retweet other users' tweets, or to flag up your latest blog or news story.

Facebook allows you to build a community of 'friends' – staff, families, suppliers, residents themselves – and keep them up to date on your home's activities – events, days out, new facilities and so on – as well as alerting them to interesting new material on your website. It's a low-cost way to build a local reputation, and you can, should the occasion arise, also use Facebook for local advertising. It can be surprisingly cost effective as you target your audience precisely by age, gender, location and interests.

Your upper sales limit with a care home is defined by the number of rooms that you have. When you've run out of rooms, you've run out of things to sell, in the same way that a golf club only has the hours of daylight available. So your rooms define your potential income. How much are you prepared to spend filling them up? What margins do you achieve on filling the last few? And can you then review your charges to new residents because you only have one or two rooms vacant?

Year one will always be different, because every new care home will need a large burst of marketing to get it off the ground. If you don't spend enough at that stage, you can flounder. Care homes don't usually sell themselves; you need to go out and do it. While there will always be demand and people coming to you via word of mouth, you as the care home owner should constantly be looking to be as close to capacity as possible.

There is inevitably a delayed reaction to you spending money and effort on marketing. Building up a reputation can take a long time, and not everyone is looking for a care home place immediately, but instead may be researching future options, so here you are fuelling future leads.

Step 3: How many marketing techniques?

An analogy I use when discussing marketing is the humble kitchen table: how many legs does it need to stay upright? The minimum is three, but four is desirable. But if you really want to make it sturdy, you might add even more legs than that.

The 'legs' in this analogy are the components of your marketing campaign. When you're planning what to do (either to launch or to sustain your business), sit down and come up with twenty-five or more ideas. Write them all down, from the obvious through to the wild and wonderful. Some of the wackiest might cost little or nothing in terms of time or money, but will get your name about in a positive way, so they deserve to be included. Your extra 'legs' can be removed and replaced at any time – don't be afraid to change them around, and remember that it's OK not to succeed occasionally, as long as you learn from any failures.

There will always be three or four musts in your marketing armoury, or 'legs' on your imaginary table, and these are usually a good website, printed collateral, PR and social media. Keep those main ones in place at all times, and you can then try others to see which work best and generate interest. These other options could include leaflet drops in a given area, ads in local papers or county magazines, Facebook advertising or Google AdWords, putting up ads in shops or local businesses, sponsoring a local 50+ club's activities, holding open days with interesting activities going on. . . the list is endless.

Making the offer of 'try before you buy' worked well for me – encouraging people to take respite care for a week (allowing their family a much-needed break from caring to spend a few days away, perhaps). That helped lower the barriers which many elderly people had when the right time came for them to go into full-time care.

In the lead up to our launch, we ran successful open days so that local people could see for themselves what their options might be further down the line. No one should go into care before they want or need to, but having some plan of where they'd like to go in advance, rather than making a choice in a hurry following a fall or discharge from hospital, can avoid people making hasty and ill-informed decisions.

At the end of the day, for every business, generating leads is all about ROI (return on investment). And it's vital here to differentiate 'expenditure' from 'investment' – one will maintain your business, the other will project it forwards. If a new potato peeler in the kitchen will save you money through reduced staff costs, or a new intercom system will save staff having to walk so many miles in a day, it's not expenditure, it's an investment. If taking on an extra member of staff will more than pay for itself by reducing your agency fees, it's not expenditure, it's an investment. And it's exactly the same with marketing and sales work that generates increased revenues and profits for your business.

Step 4: Converting your leads

Generating leads is one half of the equation, but unless you convert a proportion of those into sales, you are wasting your time and money.

My experience is that lead conversion shouldn't be just an afterthought in a care home, something that is dealt with by whoever's available when someone turns up for a viewing. It should be a separate department and properly staffed, managed and funded. The department's job is to take your expensively generated leads and turn a certain percentage into sales. I recognise that having someone dedicated to marketing and sales diverts from most care home structures. But it is key to your profitability.

I worked backwards from the position of how many care places I needed to fill in a year, and how many leads I knew (from experience) that I had to generate to fill those places. Then I could calculate how much it was worth spending on generating those leads.

Winning £1 million of new business in a year – as I needed to – represents a significant challenge, even if some of that will come to you through recommendations or simply because you are one of a limited number of homes in a given area.

Ensuring that you raise the conversion rate to its highest possible ratio is all down to making sure you get the right information to people so they know what to expect even before they arrive, and that you don't overpromise and underperform. And every lead has to be worked hard with its own standard operating procedure, dealt with promptly, followed up if necessary in a timely way, given a viewing they will remember and followed up again if needed. Showing someone around a care home, going through the interview to elicit what really matters to the family or resident and closing a sale is a real skill.

Sales and marketing is the business converted into numbers.

Takeaways

- Don't view marketing as an expenditure, but as an investment which will make you more profitable – and make sure it's done professionally and measured.

- It's filling the last few places in a care home that will often determine its profitability, so never take your foot off the marketing pedal.

- Sales leads can sometimes take a long time to convert into business, so be prepared to keep leads warm through helpful and interesting newsletters, social media and emails.

- Driving traffic to your website is critical. Apply the principle of content marketing and populate it with informative material which will give a positive impression to visitors and help your search engine optimisation (so putting you higher up the search rankings). Testimonials are particularly valuable.

- Converting hard won leads is essential. Make sure you have the right people in place and the right resources to handle visits.

CHAPTER 5

Delivering The Promise

I sold my care home in Essex to Care UK within two years of opening it and approximately doubled my original investment. I can't guarantee that anyone following my advice and experience in this book will replicate that success, but I do know that the way I did it – to design and build the home from scratch – provided the opportunity to maximise my return on investment.

That said, there are challenges to face. For instance, raising money can often be both stressful and hard work. In my earlier days in business, I sometimes found myself losing the money I'd built up because I wasn't sufficiently organised in my financial dealings. Deals didn't always make the return they should, or I had to borrow at rates of interest that ruled out making a decent profit.

Fortunately, I've managed to learn from my setbacks and disappointments. Indeed, the lessons I learned from those early failures were as important in my life – and to this book – as my successes. Happily, fate took a hand just before I set out on the venture with the care home. I probably wouldn't have dreamed of embarking on that journey if I hadn't read the book which changed the way I approach business.

I vividly remember sitting at a networking event, and the chap next to me mentioned *The E-Myth Revisited* by Michael E. Gerber, which has the compelling subtitle *Why most small businesses don't work and what to do about it*. It's been a best-selling book for many years, and with good reason. I'm sure thousands of successful businesses have been built on the sensible words in those pages.

Round about the same time I was sent a CD by a friend and it contained an interview with Michael Gerber – which you could see as slightly more than a coincidence. In the recording, Gerber is very clear about why so many businesses fail to fulfil their potential, and I realised he could have been talking about me.

I absorbed everything he said. I'd already learned some of his advice the hard way, but Michael Gerber brought it all together for me as well as demonstrating how I could do things differently. I've since got to know the author who has also written many other helpful books.

In *The E-Myth Revisited*, Gerber tells a story which summarises the main points in an easily understood way. That story is of a young woman who bakes pies with her aunt, which becomes an important bond between the two. When the woman herself gets older, she tries to turn making pies into a business. And why not? Doing what you love as a business is one sure way to enjoy your work.

But while going into something led by your heart is OK, if you don't engage your head as well, you can be led into all sorts of mistakes. The woman in the story ran her business with more passion than precision and was failing to put the systems in place to make her business work – a fatal mistake because you need systems to manage every aspect of your operation.

Michael Gerber's book pointed me in a new direction. It told me that if you have the right systems in place within a business, even if you are a 'heart' rather than a 'head' person, you will be able to leave it for a day, a week, a month – or even sell it – and it will still run smoothly without you.

When I came at things from that angle, I realised the care home I was planning shouldn't totally rely on me. Which was just as well, because I wasn't from the industry and I couldn't do a lot of the work anyway. I was going to have to depend on others to do what I wanted them to do. The book was the basis of the careful strategic plan I created to add value, accrue capital, secure borrowing, accurately cost out the build, run the home at a profit and ultimately realise an excellent sale price.

I bought the land first of all, which was several acres with a motel standing on it, together with the bungalows my live-in staff stayed in. To generate revenue while I got my planning consent in place, I operated the motel as a hostel for Newham Council and provided short-term accommodation. This was very popular with refugees – not least because it got people out of the stresses of living in London, but also because I ran courses to help them assimilate into the community, including teaching them English.

I then got planning permission to build a care home there, which was where a big gain in value came, and I was able to borrow against that. As an entrepreneur, I see opportunities for a profit in places others don't. I buy something, add value, then sell it on at a profit. But the missing tools from my toolbox early on in my career were the management skills that people often learn from attending a business school or working inside a large corporate.

Fortunately, as well as having Michael Gerber's book to cement all my ideas together, I also discovered the value of business coaching, and took advantage of that.

How systems turned my business career around

In any business, you need to divide functions and responsibilities into manageable chunks in just the same way as if you were trying to work out how to eat an elephant – a bite at a time.

I start with the customer journey as the template: what needs to happen to make each step of their time spent with us – from initial enquiry through to moving in and beyond – as successful and enjoyable as possible? From there, I divide each part of the business into a manageable chunk, and each has its own standard operating procedure (SOP). And each part has a person responsible for making it happen. These sections ultimately come together as one manual for the whole care home.

So along with my vision of what would make my care home one where residents would be happy, I managed to bring the systems side of things into play. After we had ironed out the initial problems, we had an efficient, effective and happy care home within nine months of opening. I expect most businesses would take that.

At the beginning of the life of a care home, you can't take on carers, cleaners, catering staff and so on, put them all together and expect everything to meld and work smoothly. Neither can you assume that the managers you appoint will follow your vision unless you get that across to them – because they will do it their way, which may not necessarily be your way, or the best way. You may get lucky, but you may not. The way to deal with this is to work with the managers in creating the SOP, so it's as much their way of doing things as yours and they feel a sense of empowerment and ownership. They will also have some great ideas which you can incorporate.

In the same way as an owner or manager organises their business so that someone could come in tomorrow in their absence and be able to run it, so each department should function as a microcosm of that, with easily understood procedures and systems in place so that everyone knows what to do – even if the manager is not there overseeing things. To me, systemising is about asking a bunch of questions around what needs to be achieved, and working out how to achieve it in the most efficient way. Then asking, 'How do I address the key issue of communications? How can I make sure that someone who may not necessarily have high academic qualifications will understand exactly what I mean?'

It's not easy. While my original SOP manual was a written one, these days I would also invest in creating some video sections.

Even before you appoint staff, you need a hierarchy in place where the role of each post is understood. Because it's not about people, it's more about positions, and each person in each position knowing their role and responsibilities.

To offer an analogy, England's most successful ever football team – the winning World Cup team from 1966 – was managed by Sir Alf Ramsey, a man who created a system which would win the competition, with roles pre-assigned for each position. He then found players to fill those roles. Some of the team selections were questioned at the time, because they weren't necessarily seen as the best eleven players England had to offer. Star names were dropped and some virtually unknown players drafted in. But the players in that squad knew precisely the job they had to do, trained for that role in a regimented, military way, stuck to it rigidly, and executed it perfectly.

Sir Alf Ramsey picked the system he felt would deliver the results and sidelined the players that didn't fit in – regardless of their star qualities.

If you build a team around a star, the side can flounder when that player is unavailable or retires. In the same way, a care home should be able to carry on regardless when a key member of staff is unavailable or leaves.

Think how much easier it is when you are recruiting for a member of staff if the role is precisely defined, and you know exactly what skills, attitude and experience are required. You could almost arrange your care home personnel structure like a dream team – with each player knowing their position and how they need to interact with each other.

And that's what we did. When I began building my team for Silver Springs, I had the perfect carer in mind, for instance. Above all, they were kind. And eventually that person came along, and everyone I appointed after that was as close to her profile as I could get. Her values and her willingness to help and learn were what set her apart, and that's the nub of the person you need to identify when recruiting.

But care homes can be desperate – especially when they have four people applying for every five vacancies.

When I entered the care business, I was quite surprised that the sector didn't commonly run along what I would describe as systematic lines. If you look at big organisations such as the armed forces, they run rigidly to systems – in fact, they couldn't do otherwise as they are so massive. That isn't to say that systems aren't clunky sometimes, and that they couldn't do with updating now and then, but when everything's working well, every cog in the wheel runs to its own system, and that ensures it plays its part seamlessly in the bigger scheme of things. For instance, a car manufacturer will ensure different departments each do their own thing, confident in the knowledge that everyone's handiwork will meld together further down the line.

Many businesses start just as the young woman in Michael Gerber's book began, with an individual's passion for making or doing something well. But you can be so busy meeting deadlines, worrying about cash flow, developing and improving new products, winning new business and handling complaints that you start to run the business by the seat of your pants with no time to plan ahead and get systems in place. If everything is done on the hoof, reactively, your energy goes into sorting out problems rather than driving the company forward. As the business grows, small issues magnify and get out of hand – especially if you are relying on cash flow to fund your expansion, or taking on new staff who may not fully understand your way of working.

I can't emphasise too strongly the importance of the buy-in to your vision by your managers and all your staff. Getting your staff to fit in with your way of working is a two-way thing – and you need to explain clearly what you expect.

I'll take cleaning as an example, because it is some-times (incorrectly) assumed to be a menial role within the care home. In fact, it is as important as any other. Unless everyone knows what they're doing and why they're doing it, that part of the system can soon break down. A failure in cleaning can lead to smells putting off prospective new residents, and it can result in the spread of infections, both of which can rapidly bring a home to its knees.

If you haven't got guidelines and detailed operating procedures in place, staff won't know exactly what to do. And if they fail to live up to your unexplained expectations and get criticised for it, they can end up leaving, costing you money and creating inconsistencies in the service you deliver.

Recruiting and training staff

I've gone on and on about the promise a care home needs to offer and deliver on, and how having the right staff on board who will buy into your ethos and way of doing things is paramount. It follows, then, that a critical part of the recruitment process is identifying those people from the very start, not simply employing people who appear to have the qualifications, experience and references.

Losing staff who don't fit into your way of doing things is a time consuming, expensive and sometimes upsetting business, so it makes far more sense to ensure that you get it right first time. Certainly, explaining precisely what your values and expectations are right from the start of the recruitment process will allow those who feel they may not fit in either not to apply or to drop out.

The Myers–Briggs test, or another form of psychometric testing, is a tool that could assist in this process by going more deeply into the personality profiles of applicants. Doing this thoroughly is an expensive process, which is why it is usually applied to more executive level appointments, but retrospectively identifying and weeding out those people who don't fit in can be expensive too, especially when you consider the damage they can cause the home while they are working there.

While the people we let go from Silver Springs were perfectly well qualified and had all been employed in care homes before (and probably since), they didn't share my vision of what good care looked like, or feel comfortable with doing things my way.

We eventually started advertising for staff using wording that was different in emphasis, and 'hospitality' rather than 'caring' led. That way we attracted people who weren't currently carers, but whom we believed we could train to fill those roles simply because they were patently kind and compassionate. We ran a series of open days where anyone could simply drop in and see what we were all about in a relaxed way, and this worked well. We got some good people who had no baggage or preconceptions of what caring was, but wanted to know more – encouraged by how we described our home and our philosophy. And that's important, because working in a care home carries with it some negative preconceptions. If you can alter that negativity, you may get some different applicants coming through the door.

Once they are on board, retaining the best staff is critical – they cost a great deal to recruit. Part of making sure you retain them is ensuring that their job doesn't become so routine that residents become merely numbers to them. Management has a responsibility to maintain motivation and recognise that everyone is an individual. We would refresh our employees with extra training and so on, and empower them with projects which they could design as well as deliver.

As I mentioned earlier, working with our teams to develop rotas that fitted as far as possible with their lives made a massive positive difference to the way they felt about their jobs. Equally, we involved staff with aspects such as a choice in their food. Most ate what the residents ate, but we also encouraged them to ask for their favourite meals to be put on the menu occasionally.

As well as obvious things like a suggestion box, staff had regular meetings with me when, I like to think, things were open and honest. We always got plenty of helpful input from the Pink Ladies (aka our cleaning team) who were feisty and very much on the side of the residents, with whom they obviously built up excellent relationships. If these ladies felt that there was room for improvement, they would not hold back. This has to be part of the template for any successful care home – empowering and engaging staff, who are at the sharp end of the operation, and taking on board constructive criticism and good ideas.

Of course, a lot has changed since I set up Silver Springs, and if I restarted the process I would make a lot more use of the Internet to recruit the right staff. A dedicated website, or at least a comprehensive microsite attached to the main one, would give me a lot more scope to explain what sort of personnel I was after and what I expected of them. Depending on the size of the home, I would also consider using a dedicated HR manager on either a full-time or a part-time basis.

Dealing with complaints

Any customer-facing businesses should worry most about the people they don't hear from again. Many people won't complain to you, but then they will not do business with you in the future and may well share their poor experience with their friends and family, or (increasingly) on social media.

Ideally in a care home setting you anticipate problems, but you will never entirely prevent things going wrong because you are dealing with the human factor. A member of staff can make a mistake or be having a difficult day; residents and their families can be unhappy or unreasonable at times; accidents happen; crises occur that prevent staff being there for every resident. But you have to take every complaint seriously and respond swiftly, politely and positively – even when you feel, or even know, that the complaint is unfounded.

We certainly didn't receive that many complaints and concerns over the two years I ran Silver Springs, but I always moved quickly when we did, not least by letting the resident or their family know we were taking their comments seriously. Feeling brushed off doesn't make customers happy and you will be storing up trouble for the future. You have to recognise just how emotionally charged some situations can be. The family itself may well have been caring for their loved one until recently, and giving over that role and responsibility can be very hard indeed. There's genuine concern, too, especially if their mum or dad is in poor health – many residents will just have been discharged from hospital, will perhaps be confused and might have lost a lot of weight or be suffering from the effects of dehydration. There is sometimes going to be an element of guilt for the family, even though they will have done everything humanly possible to help their loved one. Seeing their mum or dad looking poorly and not where they feel they should be – in their own home – will always be difficult for family members. The resident could be giving their relatives a hard time, blaming their loved ones for putting them in the care home rather than in their own home.

Residents are often confused, and conditions such as dementia will not help in this. They can't find their things and assume they've been stolen. They can also resist being moved, cleaned or changed, or insist on getting out of bed without help, or wandering off without their stick or walking aid, and end up falling. Sometimes families want things the resident doesn't want, and that can mean getting them all together to reach a compromise.

Just before this book went to press, there was extensive news coverage of some relatives being banned from seeing their loved ones in a care home because of fall outs when they made complaints. I can't judge on who was right or wrong in this, but that is a terribly sad point to reach for everyone concerned.

In each business I've owned, I've looked at the complaints I've received rather than the praise. A single criticism matters more to me than a host of compliments. My key concern is always, 'How did this go wrong, and what can I learn from it?'

Sometimes the issue can be quite complex and not as it first appears. Explaining a problem to a concerned family member can then be tricky. One of the handful of complaints we received at Silver Springs concerned our dementia ward and was from a family concerned that their dad was being left sitting in his chair for too long. I checked out their dad and they were right. He was spending hours at a time looking out of a window. How could that have happened?

It turned out that because he had a nice view, he just wanted to be left alone in his chair, and (quite firmly) kept telling the care staff to leave him be. A key part of the culture of my care home was respecting what the person wants to do, but we also had a responsibility to recognise what was in his best interests and strike a balance.

We told the family the full situation and worked out ways for our care staff to persuade the elderly man to move about from time to time and keep his circulation going. It may not have been as often as the family would have liked, but sometimes everyone has to compromise.

Of course, technology is now available to ensure that you can keep a careful eye on how often someone does move about, whether they need to be changed, how much water they have drunk and so on. Using sensors to monitor key aspects of a person's wellbeing could revolutionise the way residents are looked after, particularly those who are bed-bound or confused. That technology, though, should only be used with the agreement of the family and resident, and as I discuss in the next section, it is another step again to consider CCTV which is potentially intrusive.

But I can honestly say that the overwhelming majority of responses we received were positive. That's because we made our promise to residents and their families and always delivered – or over-delivered. I can't remember any resident being moved to another home.

It often amazed me when people came to look around, asked about the level of care we provided and were surprised at the answers we gave.

'Yes, of course you will have your own room'; 'Carers come round at night'; 'You can choose the way your room is decorated and furnished' . . .

It all seemed so obvious to me. What did they think it was going to be like? People's perceptions of care homes can be truly sad – fuelled by the bad publicity that surround the very worst ones.

I remember once a lady came in looking for a home for her mother as she was unhappy in the one she was in. Within minutes, she was begging me to let her mother come into Silver Springs. I hadn't even shown her round, but from what she had already seen – from the way staff greeted her to the look and feel of the place – she knew it was so much better than where her mother was, and she was anxious that we would have no spaces for her.

Dealing with the buzzer problem

Spend any length of time in many care homes and the buzzer will soon become a regular part of the soundtrack. It is commonly the primary way in which residents, often bed-bound, can attract the attention of staff. However, when staff hear a buzzer, they don't know whether a person wants the TV channel changed or has fallen out of bed. How quickly do they need to get there?

In truth, attending to the buzzer properly is often one of the most fraught areas of a care home – even the good ones – and not least at busy times or when one resident needs the attention of more than one member of staff. A number of buzzers can be going at once. It can be distressing to hear one going for any length of time, and that (sadly) can happen all too often in situations where a home is understaffed. It certainly doesn't make a good impression on visitors, who may well be checking out the home with a view to their loved one coming in. It certainly grated on me!

Care home staff can't not respond simply because someone rings on a regular basis for minor requests or through being confused, because one day it may well be an emergency. It's also worth remembering that even a relatively minor concern for most of us can become a major aggravation if a resident starts to feel ignored. Moreover, small things can matter; when a resident's whole day revolves around watching their favourite TV programme, why wouldn't they get upset if they're unable to find the channel?

When I ran Silver Springs, the technology wasn't so readily available to provide solutions as it is today. Now there are systems enabling residents to call and get through to someone immediately, who can then use a triage system to get staff to respond, depending on priority, while also letting residents know their request has been noted.

In a restaurant or bar, an acknowledgement that customers are waiting to be served will relax them and make them feel as though they haven't been forgotten, and that they matter. Why don't we adopt a similarly courteous approach in a care home?

I am a great believer in applying new technology in care homes – as long as it is done unobtrusively. Telecare can play a big role in complementing (never replacing) human interactions and monitoring, from sensors which detect when someone has stepped, or fallen, out of bed, through to moisture detectors in the bed and remote monitoring of residents' blood oxygen or blood sugar levels, pulse rate and other vital signs. There has been a lot of talk recently about care homes installing CCTV in residents' rooms, primarily to ensure staff do not abuse them and attend to them regularly to turn, feed or change them. I can understand the concern many families have – sadly. But CCTV is an intrusive technology, and there is a balance to be struck regarding the resident's privacy. A lot can be achieved with remote sensors that detect and record pertinent information. Moreover, I would have no problem allowing a resident's family to share the data we recorded if it meant they were reassured about the level of care their loved one was receiving.

Social activities

At the heart of every care home should be a team of people dedicated to ensuring that residents have the opportunity to keep active and socially engaged. We made a great deal of our social activities; every afternoon there would be lots going on, from bingo and quizzes through to giant scrabble and entertainers coming in. We also had an arts and crafts room, where residents' artistic talents could flourish.

The facility to do all this should be part of the care home design. We had a number of smaller lounges as well as an area large enough to accommodate every resident, and all of them were in regular use. All too often you see communal lounges in care homes which look very nice but are empty and serving no useful purpose. Asking residents what *they* want to do is central to making these spaces a success, not simply wheeling out all the usual activities.

Many will have been involved in great organisa- tions such as the U3A (University of the Third Age) in their retirement years, and be keen to continue pursuing hobbies and interests. Offering a well- stocked library is easily achieved, and so too is having facilities to play music and host dances.

Having musical instruments available can add to the fun, too. There are some wonderful volunteer groups who go into care homes and organise musi- cal sessions such as 'Singing for The Brain', or run reading groups.

These are all obvious activities, but asking residents what *they* would like to do could easily elicit some much more interesting ideas, whether it's housing a resident's model train set, or setting up a care home choir. And if you don't have the expertise in-house, tap into your local volunteer groups. There are huge benefits in extending a welcome to the local community – making the care home a social hub where elderly residents in the area can come and join in the activities, helped by neighbourhood volunteers where appropriate.

Many local communities have now lost their social hubs and the funding that goes with them thanks to cutbacks. Using the care home as a village hall or community resource advertises it to the next generation of residents and their families. Running it as a respite facility, or as an outreach care resource, can also embed it into the surrounding community.

We encouraged our residents to take an active part in tending our gardens, and this proved very popular. Having raised beds allows those who are still able to plant and prune, while others can be encouraged to select plants and bulbs.

There is also great work being carried out in some care homes encouraging residents to use computers – especially for apps such as Skype and Facebook which keep families and old friends in touch. Every home should at least have the facilities and trained staff to assist residents to get online.

One of the top priorities in my next care home will be an in-house cinema with a large screen TV where we will have regular film showings of residents' choices, not forgetting sports events and popular TV shows.

Getting the most from your staff

When you've carefully recruited and trained your staff, and they're working well, now it's up to you to retain them. And you do that by looking after them. Yes, money is important, and I always paid my personnel slightly above the local rates, helping to recruit and retain the best people. But I worked hard to make them feel appreciated, too.

There was very little churn towards the end of the time I ran the home, and that made me feel I had succeeded in my aims. As well as keeping my best people, when I needed to I was able to recruit new ones with the right values once I had established the correct way to do that.

Introducing rotas that fit round your staff is the single biggest recommendation I can make regarding staff retention. Recognise that they have lives outside of work, and if you do collaborate on that issue you will achieve a far happier staff room and infinitely better attendance rates. You won't get people mysteriously being ill one day but making a miraculous recovery the next day, simply because they haven't been able to accommodate something important in their life.

Staff rooms should be comfortable and pleasant, with shift rotas clearly displayed (for transparency). They should also be big enough for your personnel to relax on their breaks – not feel as though they are being squeezed into a broom cupboard next to the boiler. If I developed a new home now, I would actually create an outside area or cabin, letting staff get a proper break away from the very testing work every carer has to undertake, but ensuring they're able to get back to the home quickly if an emergency arises.

Operating manuals are another keystone in keeping your staff pointing in the right direction. Importantly, precise, clear instructions on each aspect of their job can take away the anxiety some people may feel – every member of your personnel will know exactly what they need to do. I would go further by enabling them to co-create the manuals, giving them a sense of ownership and discouraging them from bucking against the system and making it valueless. Each of the manuals I created for the individual teams was a walk through their daily work so they knew what was expected of them by residents at every stage.

All that said, personnel need to know that if they don't follow your instructions, it will rapidly come to light. You can't simply assume that they've dispensed the right amount of every medicine on time to every resident. The Care Quality Commission, for instance, doesn't take your word that you have done things properly, so taking the word of your staff may not be enough for you either. Systems need to be in place to ensure vital areas like this are properly monitored and recorded for everyone's safety and peace of mind.

The care industry has something of a reputation for attracting low-skilled, poorly motivated people in some of its roles, which is hardly surprising when so many are paid the minimum wage. But part of the recruitment process has to be taking on people prepared to work enthusiastically as part of a team and accept their responsibilities. Some will always find it difficult to follow systems, so explain to staff why this works best for them and everybody else. They are a small cog in a bigger machine – and if their cog goes in the opposite direction to everyone else's, the whole machine can quickly grind to a halt.

A warm reception

How should you welcome someone to your care home? I ask that question because everything starts from there, and if you don't get it right, it can all end there as well.

I always asked my staff to put themselves in our customers' shoes and imagine their journey to make them feel at home, from the moment they or their family looked around the home on to their first day with us and then beyond. It wouldn't just happen – we looked to make it happen in a memorable way.

We had a very high conversion rate, and I would take it seriously if someone didn't book, wanting to know why not. Finding out why people say no can be as important, or even more so, as understanding why they say yes. It gives you the opportunity to up your game or rectify shortcomings.

Price can be a decisive factor. And while you shouldn't paint yourself into a corner on fees ahead of time because individual care needs can vary, giving those visiting at least some idea of what to expect ensures you don't waste their time and yours. Having a system in place for when someone visits unannounced is also critical if you are to make the right impression.

When it came to a new resident's first day with us, we went to a lot of trouble to settle them in quickly and make sure everyone in the home knew them and what their needs and aspirations might be. We even arranged a visit from each head of department so that they got to know that person – including the chef, to make sure the new resident got meals they wanted early on.

It's like a pilot checking every dial before they take off. Get that right, and the flight should be a lot less bumpy. To me, having systems in place to run a care home is a framework. The success of brands like Waitrose and John Lewis, Premier Inns and McDonald's, is, in large part, due to the fact they train everyone precisely to fulfil their particular job. This approach might sound robotic, but staff can still apply their own individual personalities to their work; the systems simply ensure consistency of quality and service.

Hotels are ahead of the game in this, making sure there are chocolates and fruit in each guest's room, the counterpane is turned down and so on. Detail really matters when it comes to the care home, too. Give choices, things such as asking residents what activities they would like to take part in and finding out when their birthday is and how they'd like to mark it, and tailor your service around them.

To me, the care plan is a given. We always worked hard on getting to know the residents, often through the key worker. We took time to know their family as well, which ones to keep in touch with, which ones we needed to be careful about. We were the residents' gatekeeper.

Surveys formed an important part of the way we monitored how we were doing, and whether there were ways we could improve. Residents may not have wanted to rock the boat early on in their stay, but as they got to know us, they felt more confident about asking for changes to their routine, different meals they had a hankering for, or how often they wanted to be visited in their room. While our default frequency was every half an hour, we found that for some it really didn't need to be that often, while others needed more frequent visits.

Every member of the staff could play a part in how residents felt about their time with us – even our cleaning team became an integral part of our offer. Yes, they did a wonderful job keeping the rooms clean and fresh, but they always chatted to residents too, and that was an invaluable role as far as I was concerned – even if it meant that they sometimes got behind schedule. Our receptionist wasn't just our friendly and efficient 'front of house', she came to know all the residents and their families too, and made everyone feel welcome.

When you appoint a cleaner, they need to be caring and personable, because they interface with the residents. Sometimes they'll want to stop and talk, and their rota needs to allow for that. Cleaning is a skill, but it can be taught. Being caring and personable are far more important qualities.

Accounts

Often (arguably, far too often), accounts is seen as the department at the end of the hallway, providing all the boring figures for regulatory reasons – tax, payroll, etc. Having spent the last few years in the hotel sector, I would now apply the same rigour with which I run my hotel to a care home – which is far less complex and variable.

Persuade your accounts people to think imaginatively and do more than simply meet their functional requirements, and they will give you a huge business advantage. Equipping them with the right software will help make this happen.

For many years, including the time I ran my own care home, I've wanted so much more from my accounts department than people who churn out the figures in their own way. The best I used to get was monthly reports on an Excel spreadsheet – which was not very frequent and usually too late to take action if something was going wrong. By the time I got the information I needed, it was history. A lot of businesses still run on that basis, or they only react to complaints about mis-billings or slow payments, or when the bank balance goes into arrears.

With the software now available, you can do so much more than that. You can have a flow of live information at your command which – as long as you make allowances for inputs and outputs still making their way through the system – can deliver you dynamic data that gives you far more control of your day-to-day business, empowering you to make important decisions in time to make a differ-ence. The numbers become a powerful, meaningful business tool that gives you a far better picture of your profit and loss situation. Yes, what you're looking at is still history – but if it's twenty-four-hour history, then it has to be more useful than thirty-day history.

Agreed, a care home is arguably one of the least exciting businesses in terms of figures varying from month to month. To a certain extent, you can predict in advance what your income is going to be on a weekly/monthly basis because you know which residents will be paying. Of course, the care home business will always be losing a certain percentage of their residents, but again you should have an idea of average vacancy ratios, and also (ideally) be operating a waiting list to fill those places.

But there will be variations that can upset the applecart. For instance, fees for one resident can come from a variety of sources: the local authority/nursing contribution/top-up fees from the family/care fee bonds/solicitors/standing orders and so on. A dynamic daily reporting system, rather than one that only tells you what is going on monthly or weekly, will flag up any discrepancies – such as expected payments not going in.

Nowadays there is no reason for the accounts department to run things their way. The business owner must tell both their bookkeeper and accountant what they need to know, in what format and when, and not be persuaded otherwise.

You could, to make your life simple, have just one entry for income. But equally, you could break that down for more granular information. I would want to determine, for instance, what I receive from certain types of room: premier and deluxe, ground floor/upper floor, dementia/non-dementia/ respite care/try before you buy, as well as who will be paying for it: local authority/private payer/care fee bonds and so on. Having all this data at my fingertips can help me determine if I am running at maximum profitability and efficiency, and flag up whether there are ways to improve my financial performance. For instance, would it be better for me to devote more rooms to dementia care? Should I focus on having more respite care? Can I afford to fill up vacant rooms with local authority funded residents? Am I getting more demand for premier rooms than standard, and if so, should I invest in refurbishing the less well-appointed ones?

Many of the costs of sales are fixed in most homes, making life easier. But again, by breaking down expenditure on as many categories as possible, you can spot trends and then finesse your operation and your margins. You can have more than one budget – a break-even one, an anticipated one and a dream budget – enabling you to set yourself and your team targets and keep your backers enthused.

It's for you to tell your accounts departments the numbers you need to inform your decisions.

I also want my finance people to give me the information I need in a form that I can read easily, including simple-to-understand charts and graphs. Too often in the past I've had it their way, for instance alphabetical, by code or whatever was the simplest solution for them. The technology is now readily available to tailor the delivery of this data any way you want, allowing you to group different sorts of expenditure together, for instance to compare and contrast costs and outputs.

Bring your management team into the budgeting and forecasting process so they feel they are part of the ownership of the home's success. They can give your estimates and budgets a reality check from their perspective and tell you whether they can confidently maintain the standards expected within the budget you are giving them to spend.

Getting information into the system as soon as possible is obviously critical if all these figures are going to be worth using. For instance, the days of fistfuls of old receipts being bundled into an envelope and passed to the bookkeeper to sort out have long gone. These days, purchases from any department can be scanned in immediately. I use the ReceiptBank app on my smartphone to scan receipts and then email them to accounts, where they are instantly recorded and loaded into the system. This means there is no waiting for personnel to do their expenses or account for expenditure, and you also pick up anomalies quickly enough to do something about them. Moreover, after this app has recorded receipts from a certain supplier a couple of times, it prompts you to use the same purchase codes, saving even more time.

Keeping tabs on cash flow has become infinitely easier in the days of online banking, of course. Often in my care home, we found out too late that expected payments weren't in from a client, and several non-payments can disrupt the cash flow considerably. By combining this with real-time information, plus alerts on other payments and costs on the system, you can have a dashboard giving you complete visibility of where you are against sales forecast/budgets by each department as well as across the home. You can also see where opportunities are being missed and redress that.

For instance, if respite care or certain rooms are more profitable than other parts of your business, but you aren't realising their full potential, you can explore why you are missing those targets and refocus your marketing and sales efforts in that direction.

Dynamic information like this can revolutionise the way you run a care home and ensure you stay ahead of events instead of responding reactively to them, as well as letting you know when you can afford to invest further in the business.

Takeaways

- In any business you need to divide functions and responsibilities into manageable chunks, so do this with your care home – and ensure there are operating manuals for every element which current and future staff can follow.

- Recruiting and retaining the best staff isn't just about them having the right experience and qualifications. It's all about attitude and whether they share your values and vision.

- Dealing swiftly and effectively with complaints is essential. Anything less will store up problems for the future.

- Social activities are a vital part of every vibrant care home and having plenty available is essential. Just as importantly, ask the residents what *they* want to do.

- Having an efficient accounts system should be a given. On top of this you need a dynamic system in place which gives you real-time access to every part of the business, in order to maximise opportunities and head off potential problems at the pass.

CHAPTER 6

Making A Profit

Residents running out of funds

Occasionally we found that residents ran out of money. Looking back, I would now prepare for this more carefully as it causes heartache and problems all round when it happens.

This is certainly an issue that anyone setting off in the care business needs to address right from the beginning, not least because it's a problem that is likely to become more prevalent in the future. The hard-nosed way is to ensure the funds are in place at the beginning, because you don't want to be faced with a situation where you might have to ask someone to leave.

Of course, if funds do run out, you can approach the local authority. With their support – backed by top-up funds from the family – a resident can (theoretically) stay in place. But the family may not wish, or be able, to provide back-up funds. Funding the resident's care needs may then fall back on to the local authority. Councils, meanwhile, have pre-set limits as to what they are prepared to pay (which are not generous) and your fees may well be in excess of their limit.

Even if a resident is currently being funded by the local authority, you can find yourself in a situation where that authority says the individual's care needs have reduced since they entered the home and they are no longer eligible for the level of care being provided. That can be a real business-breaker.

Care fee bonds can be a good way for home owners to be sure of their future income, and many care homes will offer reassurances around future care fee rises in return for those. From a resident's perspective, these bonds can enable them to make far more solid plans for distributing their estate: the bonds are disregarded for inheritance tax purposes, and as the resident's main financial needs going forward are now met, they can make gifts to their family safe in the knowledge that they can afford to do so. This can also assist in inheritance tax mitigation.

Yes, by investing in a care fee bond, people are taking a calculated gamble on how long they expect to need care, and if they pass away soon after entering the home, it will have proved an expensive stay. However, on the plus side it enables people to be sure they can afford to stay in the home of their choice for the rest of their life, and they can also help their families financially before their death.

So how do you turn this around and stop the question of future finances becoming awkward when a person first enters your care home?

When you start from the position of 'We need to plan to enable your loved one to be here for the rest of their life or as long as they want to. Can we have a conversation to make sure that happens?' then you are working with the family to ensure the best possible outcome. There should be no embarrassment about doing that, and it can lead to helpful discussions around long-term possibilities such as care fee bonds.

Equally, you can help the resident stretch out their resources right from the beginning by ensuring they are in receipt of all the benefits and allowances to which they are entitled – such as pension and savings credits, or benefits like attendance allowance, disability living allowance, nursing care and NHS continuing healthcare. Often a person's entitlements change while they are in a home because their health needs change, but no one thinks to apply for more funding. If a resident is selling their property in order to fund their care, a twelve-week disregard should apply if the local authority is footing the bill – again, that can sometimes be overlooked.

Asking residents and their families to talk to you if they feel there is a problem in the offing may give you all a chance to make arrangements which would suit everyone, not least the resident themselves.

The promise to your investors

We've discussed the importance of the promise you make to residents and their relatives. But you may need the support of the bank and perhaps financial backers – and they need to understand your thinking, especially as a project can take some time to come to fruition and may not hit its targets immediately.

This was important for me, as the route I took in setting up and running my home, and am advocating on these pages, wasn't necessarily the cheapest. I invested quite heavily in areas where some homes will look to economise. I was working with an element of borrowing, so I needed to persuade my backers that I was investing to save as well as to make money.

Follow a similar route and inevitably any backers will want to know not only that you know precisely what you are doing, but also that you have a handle on your outgoings, as well as on the return on investment you are achieving. Key will be regular reassurance on aspects such as cash flow, occupancy rates, whether or not the fees being charged to residents are moving in the right direction and so on.

I worked on the principles of keeping my backers fully informed on the health of my home – in every sense of that word. I had set out my stall with them, so they knew that I was running the home along certain lines that would deliver excellent personal care, and that this route would lead to higher occupancy rates, rising fees and (ultimately) a sound return on their investments.

Making your investors and bank aware of the total picture can really matter if cash flow starts to flag for some reason, otherwise most of your energy will be spent reassuring them.

Apart from openness, transparency and financial visibility from day one, I provided feedback from customer surveys, which gave an equally important snapshot of how the home was faring. This allowed me to recognise any negatives and deal with them.

If you can get the home right from the off, with happy staff and contented residents, your cash flow should benefit. Your energy will be going in the right direction and success will be self-perpetuating. One good reason to do things brilliantly is that it makes good business sense.

Can care homes still make a profit?

That's a slightly provocative question. Patently there are many care establishments doing perfectly well. But it's a critical question as many care homes are struggling, and anyone wanting to set up in this business will need to persuade their backers that their model will succeed.

This is the dilemma for the care market: how do you provide the standard of care that people have a right to expect, charge prices that local authorities are prepared to pay and still make a profit? You can easily lose money in the care sector as well as make it. And every care home that runs out of money and closes down isn't just a financial blow to the owners, it can be hugely traumatic for all the residents forced to upsticks from where they have made their home.

From the government's perspective, this probably isn't a problem, because as the smaller homes go down, bigger organisations are coming in to replace them. But it's a road to nowhere, not least because at some point, local authorities will be forced to pay the higher charges these bigger businesses demand. The big organisations won't be pushed about, either on the cost of care or on the level of care an individual will receive for that fee. And as there will be far more potential residents than care home places, the law of supply and demand will mean the big organisations have control of the market.

Of course, at the moment it's not the government worrying about these fees, it's local authorities, which are being squeezed every which way to cut spending. Meanwhile, the worthy principles of the Care Act are being jettisoned in a sprint to the bottom in terms of care provision. Along the way, shortfalls in local care accommodation are being met by retaining elderly people in hospital beds at a massive cost to the public purse, and at no small cost to the wellbeing and happiness of the elderly people themselves.

Longer term, squaring that particular circle means much greater integration of health and care services at a local level, diverting some of the spending from acute trusts to primary and social care to ensure that people stay healthy and in their own homes for longer. Society needs to invest more in the nation's wellbeing to make long-term savings.

Currently, health and social care are run by different bosses operating different budgets. That means that investing money at the cheaper end of the social care and prevention cycle to save money at the acute (expensive) end is made far more problematic than it should be. It's classic silo thinking which delivers poor value to the public purse and poor quality provision to vulnerable individuals.

What can the care home provider do to keep ahead of these problems? Not compete purely on cost, that's for sure. My model is to run an efficient, desirable service that people are willing to pay for.

If you really want to optimise your return on investment, don't buy a care home – build one, as I did. That way you can create a business of significant value rather than taking over something operating on a fixed margin. Alternatively, look around for a failing one – I have bought many businesses over the years and turned them around.

Why stop with one care home?

You can replicate what you build, just as successful brands and franchises have done, by establishing a template, promising a certain level of quality for a sensible price and delivering it consistently. Investors will readily fund a business model that's been shown to work, and at competitive rates of interest.

The quintessential element here is culture – the magic dust you can sprinkle on the brand to make it appealing to residents and staff while ensuring standards are maintained and staff feel a sense of empowerment and job satisfaction. Just because the system is regimented, it doesn't have to be robotic. There have been a whole string of business successes in recent decades, all based on rigidly enforced templates where the staff know what they've got to do and the customer knows what they're going to get – from Premier Inns and Waitrose through to McDonald's and Subway. All are built on systems driving consistent customer service, something we in the UK have had to learn from the US. These examples are from the hospitality, food and retail sectors – businesses facing stiff competition, where if a customer has a poor experience they are likely to go to a rival and not return.

Create your first home as if it's the first of a hundred. Once you have an SOP manual in place, you can replicate that at different locations. And no manual is written in stone – if technology changes (or different opportunities arise to improve a service), the manuals can all be updated. Every care home, every business, is a work in progress. The job is never done. Constantly you need to be asking, 'How can we improve?' And this is where working closely with staff and listening to their ideas is important.

Many of the faults in the care sector derive from complacent providers believing that they have the upper hand in what they provide residents. All it needs is for enough competition to emerge where the culture is customer first and the care homes resting on their laurels will soon be out of business.

I would argue that there's no reason why homes in the future can't be run to a template, although the last thing I'd want is for the caring, personal, individual aspect to be sacrificed. Many people will go to a brand they trust. That said, while many people prefer to go to a hotel where they know what to expect, there is still scope for the B&B that does organic egg and bacon and has a friendly Labrador roaming around the house, because others will always want that sense of individuality.

To put this into context, I think there's room for care homes to adopt the best of both approaches: work to known standards and systems, plus operate with the individual touch, complete with chickens outside the door. If I look back at the success of Silver Springs, it was that combination of efficiency and personal touches that made our home outstanding – both in terms of profitability and the happiness of our residents. I am looking forward to doing it all again.

Takeaways

- No one wants to see a resident run out of funds and be forced to leave a home, so grasp the nettle early on with the resident or their family about how long their funding will last.

- You can help residents and yourself by being proactive in identifying allowances and benefits to which they might be entitled – and remember that their qualification may change with changing health and care needs.

- If you have investors or lenders supporting your venture, keep them in touch with how your home is faring to maintain confidence, and reassure them that your business model is working.

- Plan your care home as if it is the first of a hundred with a template that could succeed if you were to replicate it elsewhere. Why stop with one care home if your model succeeds?

- Depending on being cost competitive to gain market share may win you business, but with local authority fees being so low, it may prove impossible to maintain standards. Competing on value combined with quality is invariably a surer long-term model.

Conclusion

If just one prospective or current care home manager takes on board some of my ideas and makes their business more profitable, as well as more caring, then this book will have served its purpose.

If you have jumped straight to the back of the book, then I don't blame you. I'm always in a hurry, and often do the same. But if you like what you read here, do go back and discover in detail how and why these ideas could make a difference to your business.

Top ten takeaways

- Treat your residents as customers who have a real choice about where they are living.

- Excellent caring should be a given in a care home – the clue is in the name. It's the hospitality experience that will differentiate your home from others.

- Remember that your staff are people with lives away from work. Arrange a rota system around them and you'll recruit and retain the best carers.

- Decide what your customer promise is going to be, and make sure all of your staff, especially the manager, buy into that vision and deliver it, day in and day out.

- Good systems should be at the heart of every care home. Break down each department's work and run through how they fulfil their functions from the residents' perspective.

- Employ a great chef. Good food really matters in a care home, and a qualified, skilled chef will run an efficient ship and be a fantastic promotional tool.

- First impressions are vital. When a family or resident walks through your door, ensure the whole home smells nice, feels welcoming and has a positive atmosphere.

- Don't see marketing as an expenditure, it's an investment. Do plenty of it to keep the sales hopper full, but do ensure you know your ROI down to the last penny.

- Have a dynamic accounts system where you can see the numbers of your whole operation at a glance in real-time. Never accept less than that.

- Never forget the moral of the story about the mint ice cream at the start of this book. Don't tell your residents and prospective residents about the service you provide; ask them what they want to receive.

Acknowledgements

My thanks to:

Tammy Madge, for inviting me over to Australia where I was inspired to start the care home.

Ken Loughton, an Australian care home operator.

Tony Watts, for helping put this book into proper English.

All the staff at Silver Springs.

The residents and their relatives who made the experience memorable.

The Author

Michael Chittenden is a successful serial entrepreneur who has specialised in creating new property and business projects, as well as rescuing existing ones.

While this book is based on the Silver Springs Care Home he established in Essex, he also brings to these pages the experience of running many other successful businesses.

Best known now as the owner of boutique wedding venue Manor by the Lake in Cheltenham, Michael also owns several other wedding venues in Suffolk, Stanley Mills in Gloucestershire, the Royal Ordnance Depot business park in Northamptonshire, and a string of other investments. His career has been defined by his ability to identify undervalued assets as well as niche opportunities, and maximise their potential.

Social media

You can find out more about Michael on

▼ @MichaelChitt1
in www.linkedin.com/in/michaelchittenden